The first time I me[...]
"He is an intellectual [...] John
and I were very young men. Both of us were called into the
ministry with absolutely no concept of the magnificent
opportunities set before us....

Now I have enjoyed decades of friendship with John
Meares and have watched God raise up a tremendous
ministry through this man's faith and obedience to the
voice of the Lord. Such a perspective provides me with the
privilege of endorsing **Bind Us Together** in absolute confidence that the words written on these pages are directly
from God's heart to His people.

No man has given his life more unselfishly in promoting
the reality of racial unity than John Meares. His ministry
has given spiritual interpretation to civil rights. He has
stood as a giant against the sky, calling for total reconciliation of warring factions, speaking "peace" to the storm of
racial unrest. Any student of history, theology, or sociology
would be remiss to ignore the contribution of John Meares
in the lives of people in Washington, D.C.'s, inner city. The
message of **Bind Us Together** will endure. The ministry of
John Meares bears much fruit that shall remain to the glory
of the Kingdom of God.

Bishop Earl Paulk
Atlanta, Georgia

BIND US TOGETHER

JOHN MEARES

Published by

✓ chosen books

FLEMING H. REVELL COMPANY
OLD TAPPAN, NEW JERSEY

Scripture quotations, unless otherwise indicated, are from The Holy
Bible, New International Version, © 1978 by the International Bible
Society, used by permission of Zondervan Bible Publishers.

Library of Congress Cataloging in Publication Data
Meares, John L.
  Bind us together / John Meares.
  p. cm.
  ISBN 0-8007-9127-4
  1. Evangel Temple (Washington, D.C.)--History.   2. Meares,
John L.   3. Pentecostal churches--Clergy--Biography.   I. Title.
BX8762.Z7W1835   1987   87–29504
289.9'4'09753--dc19   CIP

A Chosen Book
Copyright © 1987 by John Meares
Chosen Books are published by
Fleming H. Revell Company
Old Tappan, New Jersey
Printed in the United States of America

Dedication

To my wife, Mary Lee, who for the past forty-three years has been one with me in the ministry, giving her full support, time, energies, and most of all the encouragement I have needed to fullfill my calling.

To my three children, Virgil, Donnie, and Cynthia who have enjoyed being "preacher's kids." They have made it easier for me by sharing my visions and goals. I am greatly blessed.

Contents

Contents

Preface

◆◇ Bishop John Meares is a remarkable man whose life is a miracle. He has written a remarkable book.

This book is remarkable because of its historical content. Church historians will want to read this book to put it in context of what the Spirit of God is doing and will do in the twentieth century.

This book is remarkable because it will bring healing to the entire Body of Jesus Christ. Very seldom in the history of the Church does a Bishop of the Church allow us into his heart and into his mind to see his failures, to see his grief, and to see his heartache as well as his victories.

This book is remarkable because it breaks down the barriers that divide black and white Christians in American society. Never has a man so confronted racism in his own life and his own environment in the way Bishop John Meares has.

The fact that John Meares is a white man pastoring a predominately black church in the predominately black city of Washington, D.C., is not remarkable in itself. It is the fact that he has equipped these people to be the people of God in that city. Never have I seen people—former prostitutes, people who were on welfare, people who found no worth and dignity in their lives—come to a point where they are empowered politically, empowered economically, and empowered educationally as I have seen at Evangel Temple, the church that Bishop Meares pastor's.

Evangel Temple is a miracle not only in Washington but in America. It is a showcase for other Christian churches of what is possible if people are willing to be obedient to the Word of God and to have courage to do what God tells them to do.

Several years ago Bishop Meares shared with me his vision of a leadership in America lead by God. This leadership would be made up of black and white Christians who would repent before God and one another for their racism, their hatred, and their mistrust of one another, thus laying and paving a way for national revival in America. I committed myself to Bishop Meares to lay my life down alongside his to bring this vision into being. There are few men in the whole world whom I trust unequivocally to have the Spirit of God in them. John Meares is one of those men.

This book is must reading for anyone who wants to see the journey of a man from legalism and rules and regulations to the full liberty there is in Christ Jesus through the power of the Holy Spirit. John Meares' clear vision about the Kingdom of God and the role of the Church in being a model of that Kingdom is a message that must be heard by everyone, not only in America, but worldwide. This is one of the most exciting books to be written in the twentieth century.

I commend it to you. It is must reading.

Tom Skinner,
New York, N.Y.

Foreword

◆◇ One of the extraordinary ministries in metropolitan Washington is that of John Meares and the church he founded, Evangel Temple. It is not an exaggeration to say that no church in the city has a broader, deeper, total, more relevant mission.

Bishop Meares, compassionately burdened for the inner city with its multitudes of powerless, voiceless, advocateless poor, ministers not only to the soul but to the whole person in terms of his or her total need. Multiple programs have developed and functioned in response to the broadest possible people need and opportunity. Many families have been liberated from welfare rolls as they have been motivated, trained, and established in self-sustaining situations.

Through the years, a large congregation, mostly black, continues to grow, bursting the generous capacity of a very large and especially well-equipped building and facilities. The family of Bishop Meares together with a large, dedicated, specialized staff, respond tirelessly and faithfully to the rapidly increasing membership. I know of no other situation where black and white meet as the family of Christ in such loving, caring fellowship.

Evangel Temple, in addition to its exemplary care of its large interracial family, has become a center for varied ministries: conferences, seminars, workshops, symposiums, etc., which provide instruction, training, and inspiration to pastors, leaders, and workers of many denominations from cities in every part of the nation and beyond.

Richard Halverson
Chaplain, United States Senate

Introduction

◆◇ "Dad, have you seen the front page of the *Washington Post?*"

It was 7 A.M. Sunday morning. My wife and I were just sitting down to breakfast when the phone call came from our daughter-in-law.

"No, Jannie, I haven't," I said. "Why?" She proceeded to tell me.

Hanging up, I retrieved the newspaper from the front steps. For the past few months, a *Washington Post* reporter had been gathering a story on our church, Evangel Temple, following allegations that I was "forcing" members to give beyond their means to our current building program. Sure enough, the headline "Prayer and Money" was emblazoned across the front page with a picture of me in my Communion vestments.

It wasn't the ridiculous charge that troubled me; the most manipulative preacher in the world couldn't force people to give if they didn't want to. It was that in a

13

couple of hours I'd be standing in front of my congregation, once more the unwitting cause of a public spotlight
being turned on our particular church.

For nearly thirty-two years Mary Lee and I, who are
white, had pastored a large, ninety-eight percent black
congregation in Washington's inner-city. Because we'd
outgrown the space available in town we were in fact
making plans to erect a new sanctuary in nearby Largo,
Maryland. Yet it wasn't this that created headlines. Our
growth—and our expenses—were no different from those
of other large churches in the area. It was the racial mix,
I knew, that once again was drawing hostility and suspicion.

How had it come about that I, the least confrontational
person in the world—ignorant of politics, naïve about
racial issues—should have been thrust for the past three
decades into this most intractable of our nation's problems?

To find the answer I went back to beginnings, to my
boyhood in the orange groves of Largo, Florida. For there
is an answer, not only to my question, but to the question
of any Christian who wonders about the road to which
God has called him.

1 ◆◇◆◇◆◇◆◇◆◇◆◇◆◇◆

The Prize

◆◇ As I neared our farmhouse my heart filled with dread. My brother Maurice had come out to the orange groves where I was working to tell me that Mr. Coyle, my junior high school principal, was at the house talking to Dad.

"What's he talking to Dad about?" I asked over the fear rising in my throat.

"Don't know," Maurice said, shrugging his shoulders. "He just seemed to be real excited about something."

I walked home slowly, searching my mind for what I'd done wrong this time. My scrapes usually started with some bright idea—like tying the cow's tail.

That had happened after my three older brothers no longer wanted to milk the cow and the job passed to me. Nobody told me that the cow would kick over the milk bucket when it was half-full or that she'd nearly switch me to death with her big heavy tail. Then one day I got a brilliant idea. Why not tie the cow's tail tassel to the railing of the fence? The milking went fine after that. No more tail slapping me in the face, no more spilled milk.

I thought I had my problem licked—until the day I forgot to untie the cow's tail. Next morning I woke to the sting of a razor strap across my backside. Dad had gone to the barn early that morning and found the cow's tail still tied securely to the fence as the cow wandered around the field bellowing her heart out. I got a good whipping for that.

Cudgel my brain as I would, though, I could think of nothing I'd done at school that would bring Mr. Coyle to see Dad. As I walked, I rested my garden hoe over my left shoulder and breathed in the rich fragrant scent of the citrus groves. The sweet smell of oranges and tangy lemons warmed by the hot Florida sun enveloped me like a cocoon. I loved the smell of the groves. On our nursery, my job was to do the hoeing around the trees and the plants. I'd spent six of my twelve years working in these groves, watching the trees grow. When I wanted the solitude of a quiet place to think or pray, I came here to the orange groves.

As I walked, I put my right hand in my pocket and felt the quarter Dad had given me earlier that day. The quarter was a reward for not wanting to go to the county fair. The truth was that I wanted to go to that fair more than anything.

Earlier in the week, the 4-H Club's Future Farmers of America had entered my green peppers in the fair for a prize. Those peppers were my pride and joy. For weeks I'd watched over them, watered and hoed them as they grew into plump, big green bells. But when I told Dad about the fair he had quietly reminded me that our church denomination frowned on our attending worldly events like county fairs, movies, or school sporting events. I couldn't go.

Every evening this week I'd listened in wonderment to the distant sound of organ music. The white glow of the lights shone above the wall surrounding the fairgrounds five miles away. What could they be doing behind those walls? It must be something evil for the church to forbid it.

I was captivated by the aura of secrecy surrounding the fair. But I didn't dare let anyone know. During the day when I walked past the entrance gates to the fairgrounds, I stared straight ahead too frightened to even peek inside.

Our family were Pentecostals. Though the preacher spoke about a loving God, it seemed we struggled end-lessly to keep Him happy. No one in our denomination would dream of smoking tobacco, drinking alcohol, or going to a dance. Though football was a favorite pastime for other boys in our community, my three older brothers and I had never played it, nor even attended a baseball game.

My non-Pentecostal classmates called us "holy rollers." Over the years this isolation from my peers had created a deep loneliness in me, as well as a hefty inferiority complex to go along with it. I loved my church and knew Jesus as my Savior, but I didn't understand why I had to be different from the other boys.

Mr. Coyle's car was gone by the time I reached our house. As I laid my hoe on the front porch, I heard the voices of my father and my oldest brother, Paul. They were talking about me.

"He won it fair and square. Mr. Coyle said so. You've got to let him go," Paul was saying as I walked into the living room.

Dad was dressed as usual in bib overalls, a straw work hat pushed back on his head. He caught sight of me and held up his hand for silence.

"Paul, we'll talk about this later," he said. Then he

walked past me out the front door, Paul following behind him.

It wasn't until evening that I learned the topic under discussion. My green peppers had won first prize at the county fair. I couldn't believe it! First prize for youngsters twelve years old was a four-day trip to the horticulture school at the University of Florida in Gainesville, 250 miles away. I was the only winner from our little country school. My principal, Mr. Coyle, took great pride in his students doing well. To this devout Methodist, educating young people was a ministry as much as a vocation. He was so excited when he heard the news he'd rushed right over to tell Dad, only to be told I couldn't go. My brother Paul, always my defender, had come into the house, heard what was happening and, after Mr. Coyle left, argued with Dad.

Between Mr. Coyle's pleas for Dad to "consider the reputation of the school," and Paul's reasoning that the trip would be "educational" for me, Dad eventually gave in, but not before he had pronounced a solemn judgment: "Mark my words, no good will come of it."

Even with this warning I was overjoyed. I'd never had the chance to do anything like this in my life! In the summers the whole family went to church camp meeting at the Wimoma Camp Grounds between Bradenton and Tampa. But this would be my first trip away from home alone!

The night before, I hardly slept a wink. Though it was common for us to rise early, I jumped out of bed before dawn. Morning devotions dragged that day. As we knelt in the living room, Dad's prayers and the Bible readings seemed to place special emphasis on the perils of temptation. An hour later, I clutched a paper sack with the lunch that Mama and my sisters Velma and Bernice had prepared, and began the thirty-minute walk to the spot where the bus was to pick me up.

My heart raced wildly in my chest as I hurried along. I couldn't believe it was really happening! I was on my way to Gainesville all because of Paul's intervention and winning first prize at a fair I'd never attended.

In all, there were fifteen kids on the bus, each a winner in a different crop category, all the others strangers to me. It was early morning. The gray fog lifted slowly, like a heavy curtain. As the flat, Florida countryside emerged through the rising mist, I felt I was seeing the world for the first time.

Driving north, the lush foliage of the live oaks and Spanish moss painted the landscape green. There were no major highways in those days and the ride was far from smooth as we bumped along narrow roads edged by palmetto. We sang songs, cut up as young boys do, and watched the scenes around us with the wide-eyed wonder of children away from home for the first time—as most of us were.

My anxiety melted with each passing mile. Though I was the only Pentecostal kid on the trip, for once it didn't seem to matter. I was making new friends, trying to fit in. This time I was determined to belong.

We had been at the horticultural college three days and I'd managed to keep my religious affiliation a secret. Then the chaperone made an announcement that threatened to ruin everything.

"Following dinner, there will be a movie at the student center."

My heart froze at the news. A movie! I recalled Dad's dire prediction, "No good will come of it." What was I going to do?

All through the meal Dad's warning played over and

over in my head. With each dry mouthful of food I recalled his prayers the morning I left. At twelve years old I understood at last the power of temptation. It wasn't just the film, which I yearned to see. If I refused to go, I'd once again be an outsider, a holy roller peeking through the window of life, watching everybody else on the inside. All the kids would know I was a Pentecostal. But if I went to the show, I'd feel so guilty I wouldn't enjoy it. I wouldn't even be surprised if the Rapture took place, and the Lord came back for His people and left me sitting in the movie house.

All through dinner, it seemed as if my new friends were scrutinizing me. I tried to remain calm outwardly. Inwardly, though, my spirit anxiously sought for an answer. Was this what it meant to be a Christian? Was this the way other Christians felt, always guilty? Always questioning everything you did or wanted to do?

As the dining hall cleared, I emptied my tray into the garbage bin and trailed after the other kids. Then one of my new buddies came dashing back to me.

"John, it's a war movie!" he said excitedly. "With airplanes and shooting and everything!"

That did it. Twelve years of home and church training were left behind as I trooped with the other boys into the student center. It was the first time I had knowingly gone against my denomination's teaching.

It would not be the last.

2

Growing Up Pentecostal

◆◇ "See you later, Emerson." I steered my Indian Scout bike away from the newspaper office and started on the seven-mile trip home. The sun peeked up over the horizon as I wheeled the motorcycle into our shed. My best friend Emerson Whittaker and I had just pulled another all-nighter working on the town's weekly newspaper. We did almost everything on that paper: typesetting, makeup, printing. On Thursdays—press night—we folded the papers, addressed the mailing labels, put them into the mail.

Friday mornings we got home at daybreak, giving us just enough time to wash and clean off the printer's ink before heading for class at Clearwater High School.

It was 1938. Jobs were scarce and we felt proud to be working. Two years earlier, Dad had given me special permission to get a job, providing I also did my home chores. That's how I came to work on the paper all through high school. Though the work was tiring, the rewards were worth it. Working gave me a great reason to give the other guys for not playing football. And I'd been delighted when I'd been able to save enough money in the tenth grade to buy myself a brand-new Indian Scout motorcycle and join my brothers dirt-bike racing.

Now it was the last semester of my senior year. I knew what I was going to do after graduation that June. Over the years following our graduations from high school, Dad had given each of his kids the option to attend a year of Bible school, at his expense. My two sisters and Paul had gone to Bible school and I'd decided I would too—though what I really wanted to do, eventually, was join the family business and work in the nursery.

Throughout central Florida, my family was respected as civic and religious pioneers. In our community it was well-known that Grandpa Meares had captained the first schooner steamship to travel between Key West, Florida, and Havana, Cuba, thus opening up a whole new trade route. As a result of Grandpa's influence, Dad loved the sea and had worked as a commercial fisherman before he married and became a nurseryman.

Eventually Dad became one of the early Florida citrus-growers. But despite his skill as a nurseryman, Dad never lost his gift, or love, for fishing.

During the Depression, he fished enough to feed us and several other families in the Indian Rocks community. Many nights Dad would throw his cast net into the back of the truck and take us boys to the bay to fish. Dad could cast a net like no other man I ever saw. The fishing net was about sixteen feet across, heavy and cumbersome. But in Dad's hands it soared through the air like a feather, reshaped itself to fit neatly between pilings ten feet apart, and never hit a snag. We'd fish three or four hours before heading home with bags of fish of every kind. On the way we'd always stop by Grandma and Grandpa's house, as well as at some of the neighbors', to give them a mess of fish.

In Largo, Florida, where I was born, my father, Richie Meares, was respected as a hard-working businessman and a pillar of the Pentecostal church. Working under a hot Florida sun, Dad built the Indian Rocks Nursery into one of the largest in central Florida. I would have to wrap my bare feet in wet burlap sacks to protect them from the burning sand as I worked in the fields. We grew thousands of citrus trees, planting acres and acres of juicy oranges, tart lemons, tangy grapefruit groves. Over the years our family also planted palm trees by the thousands along the winding causeways that connected the cities. Those palm trees grew to be fifty feet tall and spanned the Florida coastline like lush green umbrellas.

By the standards of the day we were well-off financially. Before electricity was available, Dad installed in our house the only carbide gas lighting system around. We were ambitious, used to getting ahead in life. We were also very religious. We began each day on our knees in family prayer. Each meal was an occasion for rejoicing and thanksgiving as Dad read the Bible and led prayers in his deep, resonant voice.

Dad had been raised in the Methodist Church, where he developed a deep love and reverence for God. At the turn of the twentieth century, sporadic outpourings of the Holy Spirit occurred in towns throughout California, North Carolina, and Florida, baptizing believers in the Holy Ghost with the gift of unknown tongues. The Methodist Church taught that the Holy Spirit was present in the believer's life at the time of his conversion, with a second work of grace called sanctification. Therefore, when this new group of tongues-talking zealots expressed their belief that speaking in tongues was the only reliable evidence that a believer had received the Holy Spirit, the conflict began. Eventually the tongues-speakers were excommunicated from Methodist churches for their heresy. They formed their own fellowships and called themselves Pentecostals.

My father, Richie Meares, was among those early spiritual seekers caught up in the movement. If the baptism of the Holy Spirit would give him a better understanding of God, then it was the baptism he wanted. In a Holiness camp meeting in Durant, Florida, Dad found the two spiritual anchors he was seeking—the baptism of the Holy Spirit and Sylvia Sherman, the petite brunette who became his wife.

Mama had already received the baptism. Some people say she was the first person in the state of Florida to speak in tongues. Several of her brothers were pioneer preachers in the movement and one brother would later head our denomination.

After they were married, Mama and Dad helped found the little Pentecostal church located five miles from where we lived in Largo. Dad became a deacon and when children arrived, he and Mama taught us the value of hard work and serving God. Two things we could count on plenty of—chores and churchgoing.

Each week, the family attended five church services faithfully: Sunday school, Sunday morning and evening worship, Wednesday night prayer meeting, and Friday night youth service. Healing by prayer and the laying on of hands were as common in our house as saying grace before eating. I remember the time Paul got a gash above his eye so deep you could see his skull. Dad washed the cut off, put cotton and tape over it, and prayed. We didn't think any more about it. Of course Paul got well.

Or the time my brother Virgil had his tractor accident. While he was shifting into reverse, the steering wheel broke in his hands, throwing Virgil backwards off the tractor onto the ground, his legs doubled over his head. The tractor then backed over him, breaking his pelvis and leg in several places.

Though I was only eleven when this happened, I can still see Virgil lying crushed and broken as the tractor continued to run circles around him. Using a door as a stretcher, Dad and my brothers carried Virgil home. The next thing that happened will remain etched in my mind forever: Dad sent for a doctor! We'd never had a doctor in our home before. Prayer and faith had been the only medicines needed.

The doctor set Virgil's leg in a cast but told Dad he didn't know if my sixteen-year-old brother would ever walk again. Refusing even to consider such a prognosis, the family prayed for Virgil's total recovery. Week by week as we prayed, Virgil grew stronger. A few years later, during World War II, he was accepted by the Air Force, and as a pilot credited with making fifty successful bombing raids over France and Germany.

I grew up with a rich and exciting religious heritage that worshiped a transforming God. It was common to hear testimonies about long-time alcoholics and smokers being cured of their habits by the Holy Spirit. The cry "I haven't taken a plaster or a pill since I was saved" was familiar testimony among the faithful who gave up using mustard plasters and all other medications after their conversion.

But while the Holy Spirit was counted on to transform the inward man, my denomination assumed responsibility for outward appearance. In my youth it wasn't unusual for a young woman to be turned out of the church for cutting her hair short, or for a young man to be reprimanded for putting his arm around a girl. Although my parents were faithful examples of our denomination's call to holiness, there was always a vigilant elder looking for

25

some new rule to challenge them to a still-stricter standard. Such was the case with the swimsuit incident.

In the summer after the Wimoma Camp Meeting had ended, Dad would get his cast net, pile everybody into the truck, and invite four or five other families to the beach for a big fish fry. On one particular occasion, he invited a group of elders from church headquarters, who were in Largo for a meeting, to join us.

It was late afternoon. The sun was just going down, cooling off the sand. Several campfires burned with big cast-iron frying pans placed in the hot coals cooking hush puppies or grits. Dad caught the fish and cleaned them and the women deep-fried them to a crispy golden brown. We kids scooted up and down on the hard sand at the shoreline, racing each other or throwing one another into the surf.

Everybody was having a great time. We never suspected a problem even when one of the elders pointed to a group of swimmers and commented about the boys and girls swimming together in "those ungodly bathing suits!"

Shortly after that fish fry, church headquarters passed a new rule banning co-ed swimming. Most of us in our family thought it was a dumb rule. Still, as always, we didn't question it. Despite our personal feelings, my brothers and I no longer went swimming with our sisters.

There were more rules to challenge us over the years. But our family, like most Pentecostal families, kept quiet about the restrictions. I had no idea how much resentment was smoldering in my brother Maurice.

"Everybody in the car!" Dad ordered, revving up the Buick. "Ready or not!"

Everybody wasn't ready but Maurice knew better than to make us late for Sunday school. My sisters managed to stifle their giggles as my brother tore out of the house, buttoning his shirt as he leaped onto the running board of the car.

By the time we got to church, Maurice's hair was slicked back and his clothes in perfect order. Or so we thought until an outraged elder pointed to my brother's exposed white ankles and exclaimed, "Good Lord! He's got his socks rolled down!"

Anybody else in my family would have taken the subsequent tongue-lashing quietly. Not Maurice. My gruff, headstrong brother had never accepted criticism without having a remark or two of his own to make.

It was a sobering time for the whole family as the elders voted to turn Maurice temporarily out of the church for his unrepentant attitude.

"If they turn me out of the church for good, they'd be doing me a favor," my brother told us angrily. "The rest of you can limp off like little wet puppies if you want to. I won't!"

Dad as usual took the church's side. "You're wrong," he told Maurice. "Why can't you accept correction?"

But Maurice refused. For the next few weeks the whole family grew more and more tense over the stalemate started that day. We knew Maurice wouldn't give in; neither would Dad. Mama of course said nothing. As a good Pentecostal wife, her duty was to support whatever her husband said.

A church investigation later uncovered that Maurice was also selling tobacco at a roadside fruit and vegetable stand he and a friend owned. This time the church turned him out for good. The family sadly accepted the decision. Our loyalty to the church was representative of our loyalty to God.

3

The Journey Begins

◆◇ The fall after graduating from high school, I left home to attend our denomination's Bible college located near Knoxville, Tennessee. I'd never seen anything in my life so beautiful as the Great Smokey Mountains. Their grandeur took my breath away and put me in awe of the handiwork of God.

I enjoyed student life, but the church remained a paradox to me. Our Pentecostal God was mighty in saving souls and performing miracles, but I felt you could never please Him. His standards were so high. These thoughts nagged at me as the school entered its annual "Revival Week."

Revival Week was a time of consecration, a week when the students gathered together to pray for the baptism of the Holy Spirit and to renew their commitment to the Lord. I was praying hard for the baptism myself. At that time, many folks doubted your salvation if you didn't have it. And for sure you wouldn't make it to heaven without it.

Night after night, I joined scores of students at the chapel to pray for the baptism. All night long I prayed. I had "tarried" twelve years for this divine infilling, and didn't seem to be any closer now than before. But still I prayed, encouraged by the fervor and commitment of my classmates.

Then at four A.M. one morning when I was about ready to give up, I received the baptism of the Holy Ghost and began speaking in a prayer language. I was beside myself with joy. It was many years later before I understood that the baptism of the Holy Ghost was a gift from God to the believer, not a badge of persistence or holiness. An idea that for years I'd shoved to the back of my mind could no longer be ignored. Was God calling me to the ministry?

When I was a boy, folks would say to my parents, "John's going to be a preacher. Just wait and see, that boy's going to preach!"

When I overheard such remarks, I would run off into the orange groves and agonize with God. "Lord, I'll do anything," I pleaded, "but I don't want to be a preacher. I'll be a janitor, whatever You say, Lord, but, please, not a preacher!"

The summer after I received the baptism, Paul and I went to Cornell University in upstate New York to attend horticultural classes, as we'd done the previous summer. It was wonderful! I loved everything to do with land and farming, and tried to learn all I could. My year in Bible school was over. I was nineteen, old enough to join the family business. Away from the unspoken expectations and subtle peer pressures of Bible school, I would soon shake off the notion of becoming a preacher.

Reality proved otherwise. As weeks passed and the idea of ministry would not die, I went to the groves to pray. It was there that I made peace with God. After struggling hopelessly with Him, I heard Him tell me that I wouldn't plant trees in a nursery. I would plant the Word of God in men's hearts. My harvest would not yield grapefruit and oranges but the fruit of the Spirit.

Taking root in my heart was a tiny, budding conviction that God loved His creation unreservedly. Despite the religious experience of my youth, some inner teacher was telling me that "there is now no condemnation to those who are in Christ Jesus" (Romans 8:1). Day by day, the conviction dawned on me that Christ had paid for my sins and had sent the Holy Spirit to help me live righteously—not on the basis of my good works but in the power of His completed work!

Abraham was my model, as he is for all who embark on the journey of faith. Like Abraham, before God could fully show me His purpose for my life, I must leave the familiar surroundings of home and church, and travel to a strange place that God had prepared for me. I didn't know if that place would be literal, spiritual, or both. I only knew that, as my father had, as all Christians must, I had to make my own Abrahamic journey.

At the end of the summer, I answered God's call in the orange groves. Bill Morris, my sister Bernice's husband, found me there one afternoon, under a tree, my body bent double, sobbing as if my heart would break.

"John, what's wrong?" he asked, his voice full of concern.

I was crying so hard I could barely get the words out.

"Bi . . . Bi . . . Bill," I stammered, "I . . . I've got to go preach!"

Bill was a preacher himself. Immediately he understood that God was dealing with me. "Then go preach!" he said.

4

A Belle Named Mary Lee

◆◇ In the fall of 1941, I returned to Bible college. Dad accepted my call to preach with dignity if not enthusiasm. After mustering up my courage, I had approached him one afternoon in the orange groves.

"Dad, I'm leaving," I blurted out as I drew myself up to my full six-foot height. He stopped inspecting oranges and turned to face me. Looking into my father's eyes, I felt like a young boy asking to get his first pair of long pants. (There was a rule in our house. You wore knickers until you reached age sixteen or weighed 130 pounds, whichever came first. You got long pants only when you were man enough to wear them.)

"Son, where are you going?" Dad asked, his steady gaze never changing expression.

I swallowed hard. "I've got to go preach."

Dad cleared his throat. For a moment I thought I saw a glimmer of light dancing in his eyes, then it faded.

"Well, son, if you've got to, then you've got to," he said

quietly. "But personally I don't think you'll make much of a preacher."

Tuition for my second year at Bible school was paid by an older cousin, Wilmon Smith, whose family were successful dairy farmers in the area, and with whom I had talked often that summer about my decision.

Later I learned the reason for Wilmon's generosity. He, too, had felt the call to preach but like me had resisted it. Now he struck a bargain with God: *Lord, I'll help send John, and we'll call it even.*

It worked for a while, but eventually my cousin gave in and became a minister too.

Early that second year I began to fancy myself as an evangelist. To get practice preaching, some of my schoolmates and I traveled to nearby states and held revivals. My buddy Jack Crawford and I started in Blue Grass Holler, a little coal mining settlement near Hazard, Kentucky.

Miners are a curious breed. Close-mouthed and clannish, they don't take much to strangers. Jack and I found an abandoned building, cleaned it up, and made preparations for a week-long meeting. No more than a handful of people attended services that whole week and my first sermon lasted about five minutes. At the end of the week, Jack and I split the collection for a total of $1.75 apiece.

Still, we fared better than another Bible school buddy holding a revival in a holler over the mountain. One morning Charles burst through the door of the place where Jack and I were staying, so short of breath he could barely talk.

"John, I . . . I've been run out of town!" he gasped. "Two moonshiners. . . . Will you go and get my suitcase for me?"

Right then I learned that a preacher faces challenges spreading the Gospel.

My biggest challenge that year came in a little community in Pennsylvania, and this time the issue wasn't moonshiners but Catholics.

Back in those days, Pentecostals were as hard on Catholics as Catholics were on everybody else. We both had dogmatic ideas about the "true Church," and this coal mining valley was ninety-five percent Catholic. That knowledge didn't stop me from vowing to knock on every door in the village to get people to come to my revival.

I spent hours going from door to door, flashing a big grin as I introduced myself. All went according to plan until I came to the house of the parish priest. For a moment I hesitated. How could I invite a priest to come to church to get saved? But I'd made a vow.

I knocked softly on the door. After a long wait it opened and the elderly priest stood in the doorway.

"Can I help you?" he asked kindly.

"Ah, yes . . . I'm here about the Lord," I stammered. The old priest never flinched.

"Do come in," he said.

For the next half-hour that wise old priest listened patiently as I told him that Jesus Christ died to save us from our sins and how we could get saved. Once rolling I seemed helpless to stop. The priest listened so courteously and was so nice to me that I felt painfully my own rawness and inexperience.

All the next day I prayed and fasted for God to give me a sermon for this town. By the time I left for church that night, I was confident that I had a soulwinning message.

However, nobody heard it. An hour before the time I'd announced, I went to the vacant store building I had secured and built a fire in the coal stove. Slowly the room warmed up. No one came. I sang a few songs. Still no one came. Finally I began my sermon, preaching for all I was worth. With each dramatic emphasis, I heard an old hunting dog howl outside the door. Maybe he enjoyed the preaching.

When Christmas vacation came around I didn't have the money to go home to Florida. So I readily accepted Jack's invitation to spend Christmas with his family in Tennessee. Neither one of us had a car, so we hitchhiked the hundred miles to the town nearest Jack's home and walked the rest of the way.

With its forests and mountain valleys, Tennessee was nothing like the flatlands of Florida. I loved to wander through the woods, breathing in the crisp mountain air. Jack's family lived 'way out in the country. At night the stars seemed so close you could almost reach out and grab a handful. In the evenings after supper, Jack and I would go for a walk to talk about the Creator and about our dreams. On one of these evenings Jack heard something off in the distance.

"Listen up, John. What do you make of that?" he asked, stopping. For a moment I heard nothing but the rustling of the wind, then the husky baying of a couple of dogs. As the dogs got closer, I could also make out the voices of people talking.

"Sounds like a hunting party," I guessed.

"But there's something else. Listen," Jack said.

Again I strained to hear. Sure enough, mingling with the baying of the dogs and the men's voices was the lilting sound of ladies singing. As we drew closer to the hunting party we made out the melody of an old Christmas carol.

That was how I met Mary Lee Bell—on a possum hunt! Actually I vaguely remembered meeting her once before, at a Florida camp meeting when she was thirteen years old. She'd been a shy little girl, all angles and joints then, nothing like the pretty young lady I now saw in the

34

moonlight. Mary Lee was a member of a Pentecostal girls' quartet that toured the country singing at revivals and conventions. They even spent one week singing at Aimee Semple McPherson's church in Los Angeles, the largest Pentecostal congregation of the day.

Several months after that chance encounter in the Tennessee hills, I saw Mary Lee Bell again. It was the church's annual General Assembly in Birmingham, Alabama. Several thousand people from across the country were attending and Mary Lee and her group were scheduled to sing.

During the conference, I tried to talk to her several times but she was always too busy. Worse still, I discovered that she'd recently become engaged. Finally, I convinced her to see me for just five minutes.

"How can five minutes hurt?" I asked innocently.

"I'll see you backstage after we get through singing tomorrow afternoon," she agreed.

The next day on a sudden inspiration, I went off in search of my friend Walter Pettit.

"Walter, let me borrow your car!" I yelled. "Now!"

No explanation asked, Walter tossed me the keys to his new car, parked outside the auditorium.

I was waiting for Mary Lee when she came offstage.

"Why don't we walk outside where there aren't so many people?" I suggested.

She looked around at the stage hands and others milling around, and then followed. Outside, I walked her casually to Pettit's car and opened the door.

"Let's sit here out of the sun," I said, noting the look of surprise on her face. It was just the response I wanted. After seating her in the car, I walked around to the driver's side, stopping to hand an envelope to a girl heading into the auditorium.

"Would you see that this gets to the Bible School girls' quartet?" I asked.

Inside the envelope a note read, "Mary Lee has been kidnaped. Will bring her back shortly. John."

Then I started the engine and roared off. For a moment Mary Lee looked around in silence as if she couldn't believe what was happening. Then she found her voice.

"John, let me out of here," she cried. "Take me back."

"You're kidnaped," I told her.

I drove her to the top of a famous tourist site, Iron Mountain. There I stopped the car, faced her, and told her of my admiration for her. She protested that she was engaged and that my behavior was boorish, but at the same time she seemed to enjoy the afternoon. I sure did.

Mary Lee's fiancé turned out to be an aggressive, talented, handsome guy who was an up-and-coming evangelist in our denomination. To make things worse, he was a wonderful singer, an eloquent preacher, and a person with immense zest for life. Everybody liked and respected this guy and we all knew that he was going places.

In comparison, I didn't have a chance. I felt inferior, shy, and didn't have two dimes to rub together.

In the fall of 1942, my state overseer appointed me youth director for the state of Michigan. This entailed visiting the various churches and talking to the young people, and also recruiting students for our Bible college. I must have been persuasive, since more than 130 young people from Michigan registered to attend the following year. In turn, for getting so many to go, I was given a scholarship for the coming school year.

That Easter I decided it was time to take another bold step. I learned where Mary Lee and the girls would be singing and wired her a lovely rose corsage with a card signed, "Love, John."

Shortly after Easter I received a short note from Mary Lee thanking me for the flowers, but again reminding me that she was engaged. "Therefore, I think it best not to accept any more gifts from you," she wrote. "We can remain friends," she added, "just friends."

Several months passed. Then one day unexpectedly I received a casual little postcard from her, right before a church conference I was scheduled to attend. "I'm going to be at the Michigan State Conference too," she wrote. "Since we're friends, let's get together—as friends."

That card let me know I was back in the running. At the conference I eagerly waited through the first evening service. My heart raced as I saw her get up to leave the platform, and I hurried to meet her.

"Hello, Mary Lee," I said as casually as possible, offering my hand to help her down the steps.

Before she could speak, a good friend I had cued stepped forward. "John, Mary Lee, how are you?" he exclaimed. "Hey, why don't you two come over to the house for a bite to eat. Some other people are coming over." Mary Lee agreed hesitantly. We renewed our friendship during the evening and had a wonderful time talking. She let me know that the next week she would be in Pennsylvania singing at a state camp meeting.

I quickly made plans to be there too. The opening night of camp meeting I hurried up to her. "How about having dinner with me tonight?" I said, confident she would say yes. To my surprise she said no.

"Thank you, John," she replied sweetly, "but I have several letters I need to write."

I remained rooted in place as she walked away. Maybe I wasn't in the running after all.

Back at Bible school that fall, I was appointed to oversee the publication of the school's annual yearbook because of my experience as a printer. I eagerly accepted since that meant going to Mary Lee's hometown of Cleveland, Tennessee, to meet with her father who would be doing the printing of the yearbook. Her father, Lee Bell, was a printer and foreman of the church's printing plant. The Bell home was always filled with people and music as Lee played the piano and gathered his three daughters around him to sing church songs.

Thank God for mothers! I might not be sweeping Mary Lee off her feet, but I did have the support of her mother, who seemed to feel I was the right man for her daughter. Once or twice a month I hitchhiked to Cleveland for these meetings. Before each visit I did all kinds of odd jobs, saving every penny I could in case Mary Lee was home and I got the chance to take her out to a restaurant.

That school year while Mary Lee was traveling with the girls' quartet, her fiancé and I sang together in a men's quartet at school. After rehearsal one afternoon I decided to approach him about Mary Lee.

"Hey, hold up!" I yelled, running to catch up with him.

He stopped and flashed me one of his brilliant smiles. *Even his teeth are straight,* I thought.

"What can I do for you, John?"

"I want to talk to you," I said, falling into step beside him. "About Mary Lee.

"I know you two are engaged," I went on, "but . . . if she'll have me, I intend to marry her. I just thought I'd let you know."

He stopped and stared at me, then burst out laughing. "John, you can't be serious."

"I am," I said, meeting his gaze.

His laughter died down to a chuckle. "Well, thank you for putting me on notice," he said. "But I don't believe she'll change her mind."

She did, though. A few months later she broke off her engagement, and on my next visit to Cleveland I took her to a Shakespeare play, and before the night was over I had proposed . . . and she had accepted.

We were married in her home church in Cleveland in September 1944. My father sent up a truckload of Florida palms to help decorate the stage. There was standing room only. I said, "I do," so loudly it brought quite a laugh from the audience. I wanted everyone to know how I felt.

5 ◆━━━━◆━◆━◆━◆━◆━◆━◆━◆

Life on the Sawdust Trail

◆◇ Our month-long honeymoon was an adventure. We'd both saved up for this special time. Dad had made a sizable down payment on a new car as a wedding gift, allowing us to travel in style as we leisurely made our way across country from Tennessee to my parents' home in Florida.

The second week of our trip we stayed in the honeymoon cabin at Lake Lure, North Carolina. One day we remembered that our denomination was holding a ministers' convention nearby and decided to attend services that evening.

It was a wonderful meeting, filled with spirited singing. As we stood around talking to friends afterward, I noticed a woman staring at me as if she wanted to say something.

"Yes, ma'am?" I asked.

"I don't know you," she said, "but the Lord just told me to come and ask you to come to our church and hold a revival. We live in Icard, North Carolina. Will you come?"

I'd never even heard of Icard, North Carolina, but I told her, "Lady, if the Lord told you to have me come, then we will come."

I explained that my wife and I were on our way to Florida on our honeymoon. "After that," I said, "we'll be there."

At the time I made the commitment, little did I realize just what I was getting into.

We arrived in Icard the middle of October. It was a little country village located in the heart of nowhere. The church wasn't large, maybe fifty or sixty people, but the problems were mammoth. The church was split into factions. Some people refused to talk to each other and those who did talk argued all the time. Even natural sisters were at odds with each other.

The pastor greeted us with the words, "We really need a revival. However, we can't pay you much."

The first Sunday I was there, the treasurer of the church resigned, admitting he'd stolen money from the church and doctored the books.

Since I now had a wife, a monthly car note, and a few other bills to take care of, I figured I had better get a job on the side. I found a job at a nearby nursery. Rising each morning before sun-up to pray, I would then go to the nursery to plant shrubs all day—something I knew how to do. I returned home around four in the afternoon, giving myself just enough time to eat, clean up, and prepare a sermon for the evening service. This routine went on for the two weeks of the revival.

But God was faithful. That church began coming together. People started asking forgiveness of each other. The church treasurer repented and asked to be accepted back into the church. It was a wonderful time of inner healing—and needed encouragement for Mary Lee and me in the difficult year that followed.

We traveled constantly, through Texas, Tennessee, Alabama, North Carolina—most of the Southern Bible Belt. Evangelists weren't housed in hotels then, but with the pastor or a church member. At times the hostess would decide she didn't want to cook, and we'd have to slip off to town for a hamburger. A few of the pastors would keep the offerings that were taken up "for the visiting evangelists." One pastor felt we were getting too popular with his people so he simply stopped the meetings midway through the week.

One of the worst times was when we arrived at another pastor's house and were shown our bedroom. The sheets were so dirty and smelly we had to lay our coats over the pillows to sleep. As soon as the family left the house the next morning, we hurriedly washed the sheets and hung them on the line to dry, just hoping we could get them back on the bed before they returned.

But the incident that nearly sent Mary Lee over the edge occurred in a tiny room with a curtain for a door. Suddenly a big Persian cat leaped through the curtain, landing in bed with us. Mary Lee screamed and broke into tears.

"I'll sure be glad when we can pastor our own church," she said between sobs. "At least I'll know how to treat guests in our home."

Cash was scarce. There was no money for new clothes when Mary Lee's dresses got too small—and she'd never learned to sew. On the other hand, I'd built things all my life—boats, furniture, whatever. I assumed that the principle behind putting together a dress couldn't be much different than putting together anything else.

"You get the material and patterns," I told her, "and I'll cut them out and sew them up. Just one thing: you must never tell anybody."

"John, they're pretty. Just beautiful!"

I had to admit they did look pretty good. Whenever someone complimented her on one of her new dresses, Mary Lee and I would glance at each other and smile.

During our year of evangelizing I was awakened to a side of the ministry I had not encountered before—the darker side of jealousy among ministers. Where was the love? I wondered. Where was the kinship among co-laborers for Christ? It was a valuable growing time for me, as I gradually accepted the fact that ministers, like other Christians, had their weaknesses and prejudices too. Somehow I'd imagined that ordination moved a person onto some higher level of feeling and thinking. Now I faced the fact that we remain human beings.

Not studies, not ordination, only responsiveness to God's Word in our hearts makes servants, as I learned from a Mexican brother who attended a revival we were holding in Weatherford, Texas.

The revival had been a success. Hundreds had come each night. People had been saved and added to the church. However, Mary Lee and I sensed a pinch-penny spirit in the pastor. This was the closing night and not a single offering had been taken for us in the two weeks we'd been there.

"I know we all want to thank God for sending John and Mary Lee Meares to us," the pastor said.

Then he introduced the closing song.

As we began to sing, I saw this Mexican brother slowly making his way to the front of the platform. He was a short, brown man about forty years old, skinny as a rail with clothes that just hung on him. Still, he carried himself with a dignity that told you he knew his self-worth and purpose in life. Later someone told me that he had walked several miles each night to attend the revival because he couldn't afford busfare.

Once at the front of the church he faced the audience

and waited for the song to end. He spoke quietly but his voice filled the room, which had fallen suddenly silent.

"We have been blessed here this week," he said. "God has laid it on my heart that we in turn should bless His laborers by taking up an offering for Brother and Sister Meares."

These words spoken, he placed a few coins on the table and walked back to his seat.

Though he appeared taken aback, the pastor recovered quickly and added his support to the brother's suggestion. The offering that night was the largest we received that entire year, all because a Mexican brother, though poor himself, had followed God's leading and given out of his need to bless someone else.

6

Three Thousand People and a Home

◆━▷ We were the happiest people in the world when we moved to Knoxville, Tennessee. Mary Lee especially liked it, since her parents were only eighty miles away. I had enrolled at the University of Tennessee to finish the studies for my degree. A newly married minister friend, Claude Phillips, was also attending the university. We decided it would be less expensive for two couples to live together, and began looking for an apartment.

The new public housing projects built for war plant workers were less expensive and nicer than anything else we could afford in Knoxville. Thousands of people had come to work at Oak Ridge, causing such a critical housing shortage that the government had built a series of subsidized homes. These houses were by no means luxurious, but they had two bedrooms, a little front yard, kitchen, living room, and indoor plumbing. We thought they were beautiful and I was determined to get one.

"I'm going to rent one of those beautiful houses for the four of us," I told Claude. "Wait and see."

The day I went to the public housing office, hundreds of other people seemed to have the same idea. I waited half the day before an agent was available to see me.

"Good afternoon, sir," I said, cheerfully handing him my application. "I need to rent a house for the next two years while I attend school here."

The agent's expression bordered on amusement. He picked up a list and waved it in front of me.

"You and three thousand other people would like a house, Mr. Meares," he said. "I'm sorry. There are no vacancies and all these people are ahead of you."

"But you don't understand," I said. "I need this house."

"You and three thousand others."

I decided to try a different tactic.

"If I find a house that's about to be vacated, but it's not yet on your list, can I turn in the notice and get it?" I asked.

The agent looked bewildered by my question. "If the house isn't on your list," I explained, "then it's already occupied. Does it matter if the occupants change as long as it doesn't appear on your list?"

Finally he agreed to "consider" giving me a house if I located an unlisted one. The next day I hit the street determined to knock on every door in the housing project. My approach was simple. I introduced myself to the tenants, explaining my dilemma, and asked if they were planning to vacate their home anytime soon. If they were, I asked if I could turn in their housing notice.

Within two days I had knocked on over one hundred doors and located three families who agreed to let me turn in their notices.

"Here are the names of three current tenants who plan to move," I told the agent, handing him a sheet of paper.

"I'll take any one of these three houses on the date they vacate."

I thought the agent's eyes would pop out of their sockets. Regaining his composure, he shook his head. "Mr. Meares, there are three thousand people ahead of you."

"Sir," I pleaded, "I need a house. As far as your list is concerned these places are occupied."

"Mr. Meares—"

"Besides, you want the best tenants for your homes, don't you?"

By now I was desperate. "I will keep the front lawn mowed. You'll never see any garbage outside."

"Mr. Meares—"

"My wife will keep the windows sparkling-clean. I'll plant flowers and keep the walk shoveled during the winter."

I left the housing office that afternoon with a two-year lease for a home.

We did a lot of shopping at secondhand furniture stores to make that house a home. We hung pictures and curtains and planted flowers. Occasionally unwanted guests invaded the premises. But even the large rats that crept inside from the coal bin couldn't keep us from enjoying our first little home.

My evangelizing days behind me, I was delighted to accept the pastorate of a little church in a railroad yard town called John Sevier on the outskirts of Knoxville. My state overseer had not been able to find a pastor for the church and asked if I would take it on for the two years I'd be attending college.

The people of John Sevier were hard-working country folk much like the people I'd grown up with in Florida. Nobody had money. Our first Sunday the offering totaled five dollars. Tithes were paid with vegetables and meat, so we ate well. Besides my schoolwork and pastoring, I picked up some money on the side by selling used cars and running a dry cleaning route across the border in Kentucky. Mary Lee worked a full-time job at a coat factory, arriving at work at 7 A.M. every morning.

Tastes were simple in John Sevier. The men wore bib overalls and work boots, the women cotton print dresses. We pastored these precious people for two years. Before we left we noticed a new pride in them, reflected in the way the men dressed on Sunday. The bib overalls were replaced by ties and suits, even though the coats didn't always match the trousers. And the ladies' cotton dresses were exchanged for polyester.

It was here that Mary Lee and I became parents. Three months before I graduated from the University of Tennessee our son Virgil Ottis Meares was born.

For the past several months I had been praying about where I should continue my ministry and my thoughts would always drift toward Athens, Tennessee. Athens was a little mill town in the Sweetwater Valley some sixty miles from Knoxville—and legend in our denomination for resisting Pentecostals. Most of the townspeople were Baptists or Methodists along with a few Presbyterians. In thirty years and many attempts, no one from our denomination had ever succeeded in starting a church there.

To visit Mary Lee's parents in Cleveland, we had to go through Athens. Each time, we'd ask God if this was His next place for us, and He seemed to say yes. Mary Lee was all for it, because it would put us that much nearer her folks. We searched and found a lot that we felt would be a good place to pitch a tent.

The property, I learned, belonged to a retired attorney. Over the years, several people had tried to purchase the property from him, but he had resisted them all, declaring he would never sell his land. With nothing to lose and everything to gain, I went to his house one afternoon to talk about leasing the lot and eventually purchasing it.

"I can't sell you that land," he protested. "People would run me out of this town if I sold that lot to a Pentecostal."

"But suppose God had plans for it?"

"Suppose what you like, Mr. Meares. There's no such thing as 'God,' so you can make up any nonsense you like about Him."

Thus I discovered that the man was also the town's most outspoken atheist. He and I debated back and forth for most of the day. Like any good attorney, he enjoyed a lively discussion. I didn't change his views on theology, but he seemed to like my determination to have that lot. I left his house that afternoon with a long-term lease and an option to buy the land.

Returning to Knoxville I told Mary Lee of my progress. We decided we would head for Athens right after my graduation ceremonies. My future settled, I felt jubilant. And then a call came from my brother Paul that ended our celebration. Dad had died of a heart attack while waiting in his doctor's office.

Dad's funeral was a revelation to me. Crusty old farmers, their skins tanned leathery brown, joined sedately dressed businessmen in shedding tears. As one by one people testified to what Dad had meant in their lives, I gained an insight into a Richie Meares I had never known.

Dad had always been stern with his kids. He was never one to flatter or brag on us. That was his way of making us independent, equipping us to set out, each one on his own Abrahamic journey into the unknown future. I was amazed, therefore, to find out how benevolent he had been to our neighbors—including those who weren't in the church.

Several farmers told how Dad had financed their sons' college educations. Others recounted that Dad had saved them from bankruptcy. "Without Richie's help I'd been a goner for sure," one man said.

One unusual testimony came from the wife of a deceased moonshiner. It seems that during Prohibition, government agents were always locating his stills. He just knew Dad was the tattle-tale and he aimed to get even.

"Jake meant to kill him and everybody knew it," she said, warming up to the story. "Then that winter Jake got bad-off sick, coughing and sweating. One afternoon he rolled off the bed. No matter how hard I tried I just couldn't lift him off the floor. I didn't know who to turn to. Then Richie came to my mind. I ran over to his house and he came right away."

For a moment the woman stopped, recalling that day when she walked into her home with my father.

"You could smell the liquor on Jake's breath from ten feet back, but Richie never said a word as he lifted Jake off the floor and put him back in bed. When Jake got well he was so grateful he started going to Richie's church."

But the biggest surprise came when the Methodist minister asked to say a word at the funeral. We learned then that Dad had never had his membership removed from the Methodist records, and regularly made donations there. Even though I never remember his attending there, my father never abandoned the church of his childhood.

I learned much at my father's funeral. He'd labored long to strike a balance between his heart and his loyalty to his denomination. And somewhere along the way he'd discovered that extending charity to people with different views was not a contradiction of his faith but the visible expression of it.

7 ◆━◆━◇━◆━◇━◆━◇━◆━◇━◆━◇━◆━

A Broken Wedding Band

◆◇ The response from others was always the same when we told them God was leading us to Athens, Tennessee. "Poor John and Mary Lee. Going to Athens."

"When I was there years ago," one old pioneer, Brother Boehmer, told me, "they tore my tent down, burned it, and told me to get out of town. John, it will be a miracle if you get a work started there."

Whether I succeeded or not, I knew God wanted me to try. I was beginning to understand that the Brother Boehmers among us were the truly faithful ones—that God would rather have us risk failure at a difficult job, one that He had ordained, than go for certain success at an easy one.

That summer of 1947, we began services on our rented lot in a borrowed tent. True to what we had been told, the neighbors signed petitions to shut us down, but we kept going. Our meetings were extremely popular with the young people who loved our Southern gospel singing and

51

our free manner of worship. Three young single men worked with us that summer, one as an evangelist, the other two singing in a trio with Mary Lee.

I began drawing up plans for a church that would seat 250 people. After all we couldn't be in the tent when cold weather came.

The altars filled each night, especially with high schoolers. However, high school kids don't make much money. Construction on the church had started, but it became clear that we were going to have to borrow funds to complete it. The problem was that no banks in town would give me a loan and I didn't know where to turn for the money. October was set for services to move indoors. I needed $8,000 immediately. I knew I had to take the step I had tried to avoid. I had to ask my family for help.

Mama had nearly collapsed with the loss of Dad some months earlier. She was sick most of the time and had to leave business matters to my three brothers. While each of us six kids had been left shares in the nursery, getting the assets out was another matter, as most receipts were plowed back into the business.

Maurice had taken over running the nursery. In desperation I flew to Florida and asked him to put up my shares as collateral for a bank loan. Understandably enough, in view of his treatment by the church, he refused to do so. So I turned to Mother. Mom was frailer than I remembered. Dad had been her whole life and she felt "half-a-person" without him. Yet even in her grief she seemed to find some hidden reserve of strength to draw from to help her children. I needed that now as I explained the situation to her.

"Mama, you're my last chance," I concluded.

She was silent for so long I began to wonder if she'd even heard what I said. Then she responded crisply and simply.

"Call a family meeting," she said.

With the support of my mother and brother Paul, I left Florida with the collateral I needed.

In October, a little more than four months from the time we had moved to Athens, we dedicated a beautiful little white-steeple church. Even though the church was filled with people, though, not much money was coming in. Now, how was I going to make the monthly mortgage payments?

Since the little town had a number of cotton and hosiery mills, and the people had to eat, why not make doughnuts and chicken salad sandwiches to sell to the workers at lunchtime?

Mary Lee made the sandwiches, while I turned the basement of our home into a makeshift place to fry the doughnuts. I would get up at 4 A.M. every morning to prepare the dough. Soon the house was full of the yeasty aroma of rising dough and the sweet smell of frying doughnuts.

Mary Lee had her hands full with a year-old son, and getting everything ready to take to the mills by noon. She was the one who did the selling.

She did so well that we decided to rent a little building and start a full-scale bakery. The baker we hired was excellent, only he got drunk so often that we began to lose money. By now our second son had arrived, Donald Dwight, and Mary Lee had no time to get down to the mills at midday. Besides, we were both beginning to feel this was not the way God had chosen to finance His church.

I enjoyed architectural drawing, so I took a job with the Federal Housing Administration drawing plans for small one-family homes. Soon I had so much work that I hired another young man to work for me. Even the local hospital asked me to draw up plans for their new wing. It was good money and good experience, but after a year I knew I had to make a choice. I could not continue to spend so much time in drawing, without my ministry becoming a sideline. I didn't want that and so, although I'd been making a thousand dollars a month—a huge sum in our eyes—I gave up the architectural job.

God was faithful to prove to us that He could and would supply all of our needs. Like the day my wife went to Mr. Wilkins' grocery store to pay our bill. In those days you could charge your groceries, and we'd had to let our account ride for several weeks. When she opened up her purse Mr. Wilkins said, "Mrs. Meares, you don't owe me anything."

"Yes, I do. We owe $135.00."

"No, you don't owe me anything. Someone came in yesterday and paid your bill in full. They just said not to say who did it." It was a long time afterwards before we learned who this angel of mercy was. Sister Juanita Williams, a member of our church, had been ironing one afternoon when the Lord told her to go down to the grocery store on the corner and pay the pastor's grocery bill.

Athens was where my real education as a pastor began. Within my congregation God placed wonderful, godly people whose lives were living epistles of His Word.

Nora Crittenden was a loving, robust woman in her forties who never missed paying her tithes, even though times got rough in her house. She had five children and an alcoholic husband who was off-and-on in his work. The mill where Nora herself worked would often shut down for three and four weeks at a time. During one of the hard times I said to Sister Crittenden, "The Lord understands your financial condition. I'm sure He won't mind if you wait to pay your tithes until you have a little more."

Several weeks later Nora came to me with a gentle and loving rebuke. "Pastor Meares, I know you meant well, but don't ever tell anyone again not to pay their tithes. Everything has gone wrong from that time we talked. I've been sick, the kids have been fighting, nothing's gone right."

I got the message too clear ever to forget. Who was I to change the Word of God?

Then there was Aunt Mary Turner. She was the widow of a prominent physician who'd fallen on hard times following her husband's death. Poor medical care had aggravated an eye problem, leaving her totally blind.

The whole town respected her and would drop by to leave her food or money. Instead of being embittered by her misfortune, she possessed a radiance of faith that made her a joy to be around. I looked forward to my visits with her.

She would conclude our little talks with the same ritual. Feeling around on a shelf for a coffee tin, she would pull out a fifty-cent piece for the church. Her generosity humbled me. After accepting the coin I always tried to place a dollar or two somewhere where she'd find it without knowing the source.

Both Nora and Aunt Mary taught me much about faith. They had moved from the Jesus of salvation to Jesus the Lord of every aspect of their lives.

After fifty years of marriage, Tom and Alice Miller were every bit as much in love, if not more, as on the day Tom pledged to love Alice forever and placed a gold wedding band on her finger to symbolize that vow. Now I was literally trying to cut that symbol off her finger.

The Millers had never belonged to a church or given their hearts to the Lord. Attending the Athens church, they joyfully confessed Jesus Christ as their Savior and began a whole new way of life. Part of that transformation was their desire to become members of the church. Our denomination prohibited people from wearing jewelry, even wedding bands. I explained this to these two elderly people who were older than my parents. Tom responded for them both.

"If that's what it takes to be in the church, it's all right with us, Pastor John."

But after fifty years in place, no amount of tugging or soaking Alice's finger in oil and sudsy water would budge that ring. It had become a part of her hand. I had to file it off.

As I held her hand and gently sawed away at the gold metal, I tried to block out what I was doing. The woman's serenity unnerved me. This ring was part of her life. What was I interfering with?

The job would have been easier if they had protested, but they didn't. Looking up from my work, I met Alice's eyes. She gave me a sweet smile and patted my hand with her free one.

"It's all right," she assured me.

Together we bowed our heads back over her finger as if joined together in some private prayer. I was hurting inside. Not because of the ring—Tom and Alice were helping me come to terms with that—but because of my own compromising with God's Spirit. Because no one had ever started a Pentecostal church in Athens, I'd been determined that mine would be without reproach. I was submitting to religious legalism, not because God required it but because of my desire to prove myself to my denomination.

When the metal snapped apart, something in me snapped with it. I felt I had let God and myself down. Wasn't this kind of legalism the very thing this particular Abraham had been called to leave behind?

In that ugly moment, as I picked up the broken wedding

band, I promised myself I would never do anything like that again. If I were ever to reach my own "new land"— the new place God has reserved for each of us in Christ— I needed to hear God say, as He said to Abraham and says today to all who would walk in faith, "Leave your country, your people and your father's household and go to the land I will show you" (Genesis 12:1).

8

The Church that Was Built by Night

◆◇ A highlight of our ministry in Athens occurred in 1950, the year the evangelist T. L. Osborne came to hold a tent meeting for us. Bill Morris, my sister's husband, was pastoring a church in Easton, Maryland, where Osborne had held a revival earlier in the year. Bill was the person who had found me crying in the orange groves the day I gave in to the call to preach. Now he called me from Easton all excited.

"John, you can't believe the miracles that are taking place!" Bill said. "Osborne says to the blind, 'Receive your sight,' and the blind see!"

This I had to see for myself. Despite our constant preaching about a miracle-working God, most Pentecostals had never witnessed healings like those described in the New Testament. I certainly had never seen blind eyes opened or deformed limbs straightened. Could this be? Mary Lee and I drove to Easton to find out.

Bill's parish was a stone church that seated four hundred. He had pitched a huge tent alongside it to hold the crowds attending the revival. The day we arrived that tent was filled to capacity. Throughout the service Mary Lee and I were all eyes. Everything was just as Bill had described it. Reverend Osborne was what we called a "Word" man. Everything he believed and said was centered on the Word. Here was a man, a mortal like myself, using the authority of Jesus as if God were speaking through him!

I had never witnessed that kind of power in anyone's ministry. Most striking was Osborne's assurance about his authority as a believer to invoke healing in the name of Jesus and boldly assert that the Lord would perform His Word. Nor did such faith have to be "worked up" by emotional appeals, as we Pentecostals thought.

Somehow I got T. L. to promise to come hold a meeting in Athens. When he did, neither I nor those town folk would be the same again.

Three other pastors co-sponsored T. L.'s crusade in Athens along with me. I had a daily radio broadcast by that time, through which we spread the news. We also bought newspaper advertisements all through the Sweetwater Valley and rented a tent about the size of a football field. T. L's reputation preceded him. On the opening day of the crusade, people packed the tent and formed lines ringing the four sides. The crowds continued to fill the tent for the next two weeks. Nothing this big had ever come to Athens, Tennessee.

On the final day of the crusade T. L. preached on "The Faith of Abraham." Something stirred in my spirit the moment he announced the topic. Was God about to move us all to a new place in our journey of faith?

At the close, T. L. asked the audience to form four lines for healing prayers. As the people lined up he calmly instructed us four sponsoring pastors to take a line each and pray for their needs. The four of us looked at each other, startled, but obediently we each took a line. Would God dare to use me as a vessel for healing? Could God use me as He did Brother Osborne?

I looked at the line of people stretching before me and gulped as the first one came limping forward. The woman hobbled on the ball of her right foot, unable to put it flat on the ground.

Lord, I groaned inwardly, *why wouldn't You let my first person be someone with a headache?*

When the woman reached me I laid my hands on her head and told her, "In the name of Jesus put that right foot down." At that she shrieked at the top of her voice, nearly scaring me to death. I dropped my hands and watched in amazement as she began running around the tent as fast as she could with both feet flat on the ground! Later I learned it was the first time that foot had been flat in years.

I was ready to pray for anybody after that. The Osborne crusade completely revolutionized my life. My faith in healing for the body as well as the soul increased steadily and I made it a regular part of my ministry. I began praying for the deaf, the lame, all manner of sickness, and God was faithful to His Word. The people who had once said, "Poor John and Mary, going to Athens," were now rejoicing with us.

The church continued to grow. We were being blessed and had given Pentecost a new image in the town—and the word coming to me in my private prayer time was that my assignment here in Athens was finished. This was not the land where I was to settle; my journey was not yet over. The place He seemed to be showing me now was Memphis, Tennessee.

I went to see a minister friend there and told him what was happening in my spirit. He greeted my desire to start a church in Memphis with enthusiasm and I was stunned when a member of his congregation, a World War II veteran, offered me the use of his G.I. loan to purchase a place to live. Their encouragement, and my own inner stirring, was enough to convince me that God was saying, "Move on."

I found a huge lot for sale in the eastern part of the city at a cost of only $20,000. I went to the denomination's state overseer and told him what I wanted to do. I could tell he thought I'd gone off the deep end. Still, he consented to have the denomination co-sign the note for a loan—"even though I think you're biting off more than you can chew."

"Where are we going to live?" Mary Lee asked when I reported the results of my trip. I told her of the offer of the G.I. loan, how we could move into a brand-new house with only $500 down.

"But . . . can't we wait until the baby's born before we leave?"

"Of course!" I assured her.

Three months after our daughter Cynthia Marie was born—joining her brothers Virgil and Donald Dwight—we left the church in Athens in the care of their new pastor, said goodbye to the people we loved, and moved our family of five to Memphis.

Folks called it "the church that was built by night." The big lot I'd found was in a residential section of east Memphis. Again as in Athens, we ran into resistance from the neighbors when they learned that we planned to put up a tent. Residents circulated protest petitions. City officials said, "You can't erect a tent on the property."

Not one to give up easily, I pressed for permission to hold "open-air meetings," as long as no tent was raised. Having secured this permission, I built a platform to speak from, placed wooden benches in front of it for people to sit on, and hooked up a microphone. I also managed to string a row of lights around the periphery of this makeshift sanctuary. The place didn't look too inviting, but a few passers-by would stop each evening. The lights got us more than we bargained for—mosquitoes! We did more slapping at those bugs than we did praising the Lord. We held our ground until winter when we moved the services into the living room of our home.

Meanwhile we began construction on a 400-seat church. I designed the building. During the day, the building crew consisted of me and a few hired hands. At night, though, a team of volunteers from my friend's church across town came directly from their jobs to spend the evening hammering and sawing. That's why people called it "the church that was built by night."

We advertised our first big revival with one of the leading evangelists of the day. We were excited on that opening night. The church was packed, despite a steady pouring rain. About thirty minutes before service was to begin, we received a startling telephone call. Fred, the evangelist, along with another young man, had been in a terrible car accident right outside Memphis. The young man was killed and Fred was in the hospital. We broke the sad news to the congregation and cancelled the revival until Fred had recuperated.

Getting a new church established and financially solvent takes a lot of time and patience. These were testing times—times when I sometimes questioned whether I hadn't reached beyond my faith.

As I said grace over Sunday morning breakfast, Mary Lee and I tried to keep the concern in our hearts out of our faces. The three children ate their breakfast hungrily, not knowing they were eating the last of the food in the house. There was not only no food but no money with which to buy food. No one but God knew about our situation.

We held Sunday morning services that day and were grateful when, on the spur of the moment, a family invited us to have Sunday dinner with them. It was only the beginning of God's provision.

That night following the evening service, a convoy of cars pulled up to our door. Mary Lee and I stood at the window wondering what was going on, when we spotted our minister friend from across town getting out of his car.

"That's Harry Kutz," I said, walking to the front door. "I wonder what he's up to."

Harry came up the walk, a group of people following him. Each person carried a couple of bags of groceries.

"Don't just stand there, Meares," Harry said good-naturedly. "Let us by."

Speechless, we followed the pastor and the members of his congregation as they stacked bags of food in the kitchen and then, when tabletop and counterspace there were filled, in the dining room.

"What's all this?" I asked, pointing to the food.

"About four o'clock this morning, John, the Lord woke me up and impressed it on my heart that in Brother and Sister Meares' house, the cupboards were empty," Harry said. "At services this morning I told my congregation what the Lord had said and asked everyone to bring food with them to the evening service. Here we are."

All Mary Lee and I could do was thank the Lord for providing in such abundance: that's the most food we've ever had in our house before or since.

As we moved on in faith, God's spiritual and material provisions continued to flow. One of the greatest confirmations that we experienced during the early months in

Memphis came from Sister Stracener, a woman who lived in Arkansas just over the Tennessee border. For many years Sister Stracener had suffered excruciating back pain resulting from a dislocated disk.

One day lying in bed, Sister Stracener had a vision. In this vision she saw a man standing in a large unfinished building with exposed rafters. The Spirit of the Lord told her that a man named John Meares had recently moved to Memphis. *He's building a new church. If you will go have him pray for you, your dislocated disk will be healed.*

Not prone to having visions, Sister Stracener could barely believe, much less understand, what she was experiencing. She'd never heard of John Meares and had no idea how to find him. She shared the vision with her husband, but still had no idea what to do about it.

A few days later, they were reminded of the vision when they attended evening services at a church in Memphis. "You should have been here this afternoon to hear Brother Meares," the minister told them. "He was here with his wife and a singing trio, conducting a healing service."

"Did you say his name is Meares?" Sister Stracener asked excitedly. "Is his first name John?"

"That's right. He's pastoring a new church over in east Memphis."

Barely able to contain their excitement, the Straceners got the address of our church and were at the front door waiting when I arrived for the evening service. Sister Stracener told me about her back problem and how God had directed her to me for prayer. When I prayed for her during the service she was instantly healed!

The family began attending our church and I was able to see Sister Stracener's transformation for myself. Her posture improved dramatically and she could stand and walk without pain. Soon after this, the family moved to California.

I received a letter from her there, saying her healing was still complete. To prove it, she enclosed a photo of herself working at her new job. She was a riveter at an airplane factory!

My ministry settled and took shape along with the new building. Ten months after we arrived in Memphis, the Park Avenue Church that was built by night stood as a monument of God's faithfulness.

9

What Color Is God's Child?

◆◇ In the summer of 1954, John and Ethel Petrucelli joined Mary Lee and me in the ministry. Of Greek and Italian descent, John had the warmth and charm to go along with his emotional Mediterranean temperament. The son of a Pentecostal preacher, Johnny was a vibrant, fast-talking fellow who'd attended the same Bible college I'd gone to. When he graduated in 1952 he was voted "Mr. Lee College." It was at school that Johnny met Ethel, the lovely Hawaiian beauty whom he married the summer they graduated.

When we met them, the Petrucellis had a small daughter, Sheari, and were evangelizing in small Southern communities. Ethel was ready to move to a large city. Memphis, however, was hardly ready for Ethel.

Converted to Pentecostalism in Hawaii, Ethel had received a scholarship to our denomination's Bible school in Tennessee. Rebelling against the school's strict rules, she was the first to lead some of the other girls to challenge the church's taboos by cutting their hair short, shaving their legs, and wearing makeup. Despite the scandalous nature of these activities, no one bothered Ethel much. Her being Hawaiian, they figured she just hadn't been taught right from wrong.

It was through Ethel that I was first confronted with the ugliness of racism. Black churches of our denomination had always had segregated congregations under the auspices of the denomination. With Ethel's dark olive skin tanned further by the sun, she was about as close as our denomination came to integrating our all-white churches.

It didn't pay much, but it was a job. The Petrucellis had been in Memphis two weeks when Ethel found work at a large department store—down in the basement in the packing department with the "colored" workers (as blacks were called in those days). Halfway through her first shift, the white foreman came down to tell her she was being moved.

"We didn't know you were Hawaiian," he apologized. "We're moving you to another department."

"No, thanks," she responded. "I'm fine where I am."

She was a spunky young woman who learned about prejudice only when she came to the mainland. Johnny drove her to work every day because, as she explained, "I'm scared I'll punch somebody if they try to make me ride in the back of the bus."

Ethel never did ride in the back of a bus. The closest she ever came was the day Johnny's car broke down and he told her to take a cab home from work. As the cab drove up to the Petrucellis' garage apartment, the landlady ran out of the house and snatched open the door.

"Get out of there," she said. "You're not supposed to ride in that cab."

The landlady could tell from her bewildered expression

as Ethel hurried out of the cab that she had no idea what was wrong.

"Don't you understand how things are here?" she asked. "They put you in a colored cab! The colored cabs are for colored people and the white cabs are for white people."

Every so often, when the Sunday evening services concluded at our church, the four of us would head across town for a late-night radio broadcast service at a black Baptist church. We all enjoyed the good music and the lively preaching of Dr. Brewster, who glorified the Lord and, in his oratory style, made Him real.

With each new experience it appeared that God was preparing me for the next. My traditional views about holiness had changed tremendously. Though I knew there was a member in my congregation who smoked, I didn't try to reprimand him. I was learning to reach out and restore with love and patience, not to condemn and excommunicate.

I'd moved to a place where I saw self-discipline as a work of sanctification brought about by the Holy Spirit. The church was to help the believer manifest that spiritual control in his life, not to be a policeman.

I now began to realize what a powerful contribution black believers had to make to the Body of Christ. As I began to see the racial hypocrisy of the church, it was as if scales had fallen from my eyes. True, it was only part of an entire social system in America, but did the church have to support the world's social systems?

It happened in a Sunday morning service. As usual Johnny was taking the praise and worship portion, leading the congregation in singing.

Without warning they walked in—a middle-aged black couple accompanied by three teenage children. No one noticed them as they took seats approximately five rows from the back except one usher, a very dogmatic brother who held to the letter of the law in all church matters.

He walked over to the newcomers, whispered something to the woman, and watched as they all got up and left. Johnny had now finished his segment of the service and I was scheduled to speak after Mary Lee finished her solo. I called Johnny aside. He had also seen the incident.

"Go after them quick and bring them back," I whispered before walking to the podium.

Later he related the full story to me.

Johnny had run five blocks before catching up with the family. "We don't want to cause any trouble," the woman said in response to his invitation to return. "We heard about the miracles of healing on your radio broadcast . . . but we don't want to cause any trouble."

With some coaxing Johnny finally got them to reconsider. I was relieved when I saw them come in the door. I wasn't going to turn anyone, white or black, away from worshiping God.

When the usher who had asked the family to leave saw what was happening, he could barely contain his anger. He was a tall, hefty man who seemed to grow even bigger and taller as he watched these people walking back in. Standing up, that usher motioned for his wife and seven children to follow him out of the church. I kept preaching as if I'd seen nothing.

Later when I gave the altar call, I thanked God as I watched the whole family coming down the aisle, tears streaming down their faces, to give their hearts to the Lord.

I knew I had to talk to the usher. That family had come to our church because they wanted to be blessed. Did God have one blessing for white people, a different one for other races?

Early Monday morning, I went to visit the usher. He had always been a faithful supporter of the church, attending services every time the doors opened. I didn't want to be insensitive to his feelings, but the more I tried to reason with him, the more rigidly he resisted.

"No!" he exclaimed, "I *don't* understand. If you want me and my family to return, you'll have to promise me that you'll never allow another nigger in our church!"

That was his final word.

"Brother," I said quietly, "I'm very sorry. But I will never, ever prohibit anyone, of whatever color, from attending our services."

I had grown up with the blacks who worked in my father's nursery. Many of my playmates came from these families. Though I had often eaten in their homes, I'd known by some unwritten law that I could not extend the same invitation to them to eat at my house.

I'd accepted the situation, as a child accepts any social norm. Now, however, I was not a child, but a minister of the Gospel. Whose norm was I to follow, Christ's or society's?

In 1955 such thinking was fairly radical stuff. The school desegregation issue had inflamed the nation the year before when the Supreme Court ruled that segregated public schools were unconstitutional. But religious politics, not social politics, were my concern. It seemed to me that God was leading me into a ministry that would be more open socially and culturally than the church of my youth.

By the end of 1954 we had been in Memphis three-and-a-half years. Our ministry had grown in size and influence and I was fulfilled with what God was doing. Yet I sensed a familiar restlessness in my spirit. Could it be that the Lord was calling me to move on once again? Surely not. Memphis was a great city, a great place to raise a family.

I wrestled with these questions, spending many nights in prayer.

Late one Saturday evening Johnny came into the church office unexpectedly to find me prostrate on the floor, weeping.

"Johnny," I said, clambering to my feet, "there is a people somewhere who are really hungry for God. Whoever and wherever they are, I want to go to them."

10

Hungry for God

◆◇ I've come to believe that every person who means to follow God must do so in fear and trembling. The future into which He calls each of us is every bit as unknown as was Abraham's. Our faith must be greater than our fear, including our fear of failure.

I didn't know anything about Washington, D.C., except that it was the nation's capital. I had never been there but once and that was on my senior high school trip. I knew no one living there, and the North had never held any attraction for me.

But . . . when I sensed the Lord telling me to move on, I asked Him where. The answer came in two parts. In my spirit, God told me that He would lead me to a people who had a hunger for Him, and—strangely—that I was to go to Washington, D.C.

One night when I'd been up praying, I woke Mary Lee at three in the morning and told her, "Honey, God is calling me to Washington, D.C."

Always the practical one, she asked, "John, do you know anyone there?"

"No one," I replied.

"Then why Washington?"

"God wants me to go."

I'm sure she didn't take me seriously as she turned over and went back to sleep. But a couple of weeks later when I told her, "Mary Lee, put the house up for sale!" she grew solemn indeed. We'd just built a beautiful ranch-style house with a thirty-foot living room looking out on an acre of trees. Tears welled up in her eyes as she ran into the bedroom and locked the door behind her. Around four that afternoon she emerged, her eyes swollen and red, but with a smile on her face.

"I'm ready," she said. "Let's go."

From the earliest days of our marriage Mary Lee's confidence in me had been my anchor and my conscience. I knew she depended on me to do the right thing for our family. And because of her trust, I tried to live up to her expectations.

I was awakened at 2:00 A.M. the following morning by the ringing of the telephone. I groped sleepily for the receiver, wondering who could be calling at this ungodly hour.

"John, it's Jack. Wake up, man!"

The voice of evangelist Jack Coe nudged me into consciousness. It wasn't uncommon for Jack to call me at odd hours to report something great happening in one of his meetings. This time, though, his news concerned me personally.

"John, you told me last week you thought you were supposed to go to Washington. Well, I'm putting my tent up there. Come up and help me with the meetings. Afterwards you can stay and raise up a church."

Now I was fully awake. In all the years I'd known Jack he'd never held a crusade in Washington, nor had he ever asked me to participate in a meeting with him. Jack Coe was known throughout the United States for his great evangelistic and healing campaigns, which drew thousands.

His call was the confirmation I needed to assure me that I was doing the right thing. I resigned from the church in Memphis. Then the following week I set out for Washington to meet with Jack's crusade director. My family and the Petrucellis would join me later.

"Hallelujah!"

"Praise the Lord!"

Nightly people packed the big top erected on a vacant lot at Benning Road, N.E. Twenty-five churches from the metropolitan Washington area were sponsoring Jack Coe's six-week crusade. Their pastors sat on the stage as Jack preached up a storm and folks were healed miraculously of goiters, deafness, and all kinds of illnesses. Word of the miracles spread, bringing people out in droves until the Park Police mounted on horseback, had to ride through the crowd to keep aisles open for fire safety. Folks would arrive an hour or two before the service started in order to get a seat.

To get the service underway, the organist would play and get people singing and clapping. The sound of thousands of joyful voices drifted into the night air while residents of the surrounding neighborhood sat on their front porches.

Gradually the music and the lights began to draw people from this mostly black area to the services. Each night I watched as an amazing transformation occurred. The number of black faces increased even as the number of white faces declined. By the end of the crusade when Jack introduced me, I faced an almost totally black audience.

"John, come here," Jack said, motioning to me.

I walked to the pulpit and stood beside him.

"Brother Meares here is a preacher," Jack said, putting his arm around my shoulder. "As you know he has been assisting me in these meetings. And he's staying here to start a church. I'll be preaching for him at his first service."

I left the platform to the sound of polite applause. Inwardly my heart was churning with the realization of what apparently lay before me. I'd been in Washington six weeks; slowly the reality was sinking in that I had come to a largely black city. My vision had been to find a people who hungered for God. Were these the people? If so, how would they receive me?

When that black family had walked into our church in Memphis, it was easy to accept them. They were the minority and they had come to us. Now the tables were turned. I was the minority and my functioning would be dependent upon the people's accepting me.

Where we started our church, in Turner's Arena at 14th and W Streets, was certainly not inviting. Crime was rampant! It was once used as a Park Police stable, with the smell of horses still in the walls, the arena now held wrestling matches and square dances on Wednesdays and Saturdays, and our church services on the other nights. Since there was no other space available, I signed a six-month lease, swept out the beer bottles, put up my portable platform, and opened for service the Washington Revival Center.

Jack's appearance that first Sunday brought an overflow

crowd to the arena, many of whom returned to form the nucleus of the congregation. Soon the Center was sending shock waves throughout churches in Washington and the Southern Bible Belt as some folks in my own denomination spoke of John Meares and his "niggers." In Washington, relatives lambasted family members for giving their money to "that white man who ain't gonna marry you or bury you!"

We were an enigma. In a city, and a nation, where racial segregation was as solidly entrenched in the Church as it was in the neighborhoods, we were flying in the face of tradition. The reality was as surprising to me as it was to my critics; I had never heard of a white man pastoring a colored church.

We sat alone in Washington, like an island. Behind my back the black pastors in the city accused me of encroaching on their territory—stealing their members and stirring up disunity. White non-Pentecostal pastors ignored me as much because of my Pentecostal doctrine as for my unique congregation. The elders in my own denomination see-sawed back and forth between reactions of curiosity and shock.

How could I explain to them what I scarcely understood myself? I hadn't come to Washington to become a social crusader or a leader in the civil rights movement. I had come at God's leading, not knowing who or what I would find—and what I had found was a people hungry for God.

Officials in my denomination gave me twelve months to organize a church "in compliance" with church norms. Between their criticism and the culture change I was daily experiencing, I turned to the two sources where I'd always found my strength in times of stress—the Lord and the people of my congregation. Both were my comfort and my affirmation. The spiritual transformations happening in the lives of my parishioners were a continuing assurance that I was where God wanted me to be.

Over the next year, that affirmation was to cost me more than I dreamed.

11

Adjustments

◆◇ Six months after its inauguration, the Revival Center moved to an old government warehouse at 1331 U Street, N.W. The big block-shaped building was far from luxurious, but much more comfortable than Turner's Arena with its hard wooden bleachers and horse stable smell.

Because we were not allowed to make structural changes, bedsheets soaked in fire-proofing solution served as partitions. The fire marshal came by periodically to ensure that they passed the fire code.

The only problem at our new location was the community welcoming committee—young hoodlums who broke windows and slashed our car tires on a regular basis. At one point the vandalism was so bad we began putting our cars on the freight elevator and parking them on the fourth floor of the warehouse. That stopped when city officials banned the practice.

With our new surroundings, we also took on a new

name, the National Evangelistic Center. The name reflected my increasing conviction that this ministry would one day have a broader focus than just this one city. On a regular basis I brought in the leading evangelists of the day to preach. Our motto at the Center was "Jesus for Washington and Washington for Jesus." A colorful banner proclaiming that message draped the front of the building. That was the theme we stressed in our services and on our daily radio broadcasts over station WPIK.

Life was good for us, though not exactly comfortable. We'd made major adjustments in our lifestyle to accommodate the move. I'd leased a house in Arlington, Virginia, that we occupied with the Petrucellis and two other people we'd brought with us from Tennessee—Harold Jackson, a Bible teacher who had been healed at one of our meetings, and my wife's niece, Clariece Miller, the organist. Ten of us lived in the house, sharing chores and resources.

The cramped basement quarters where our family stayed were a far cry from our spacious home in Memphis, but Mary Lee made the adjustment without complaint. God was moving in our lives on a spiritual scale such as we'd never experienced before; that fact far outweighed any physical disadvantages.

Until we came to Washington, I don't think my wife and I realized just how white our lives had been. We were as naïve about black people as if we'd lived on another planet.

"Boy, that was great!" Mary Lee would exclaim, meaning it as a compliment—only to be taken aside and cautioned, "We never use the word *boy*."

When we were able to move into a house of our own, we hired a young member of our congregation, Francis, to help us out. That winter we invited Francis to come with

79

all of us on vacation to my family's home in Florida. I hadn't even thought about motels and restaurants along the highways not being open to blacks. Later, church members explained that when they traveled in the South they drove nonstop, slept in their cars, or stayed with friends along the way because the roadside motels wouldn't give them a room.

The first restaurant we stopped at, Francis was told to go to the kitchen to be served, or eat in the car. We ate a lot of picnics, that trip. We would also wait till after dark to stop for the night. "Stay in the car," I'd tell everyone. I'd go check in, requesting two rooms, one for me and Mary Lee, the other for my four children. After all, I reasoned, Francis was my child in the Lord. We were all glad to get back to Washington, sadder but wiser in the daily realities faced by millions of our fellow citizens.

Within our congregation itself was immense diversity, both cultural and religious. While many of our people were unchurched folks who had never confessed Jesus Christ as their Savior, others spanned the range from second-generation conservative Pentecostals, through middle-class Baptists, to fourth- and fifth-generation Methodists and Catholics. Ours was a melting pot of faiths and social backgrounds that gave our church a unique style and vibrancy.

I got a kick out of watching Mary Lee make the change from sheltered Southern belle to urban pastor's wife. Prior to coming to Washington she had worked hard to extricate herself from some of our denomination's legalisms about proper dress. A wedding ring was her concession to wearing jewelry. A dab of make-up gave a hint of rosiness to her cheeks and a faint tint to her lips. Neither "fancy" nor "plain," she felt she'd struck a perfect compromise as a Pentecostal woman.

Now the conservative holiness women in our congregation, in their long dresses, without ornament—and positively no open-toed shoes!—were surprised at Mary Lee's "worldliness." On the other end of the spectrum were our few sophisticated fashion queens. With faces painted as skillfully as an artist's canvas, colorful wide-brimmed hats tipped seductively on their heads, fully accessorized with jewelry, and often a fur piece draped over their shoulders, they pitied the poor, plain pastor's wife.

Although she had performed with musical groups for years, Mary Lee worked in vain to adapt her white Southern Gospel sound to the church's black choir. They wanted to sing their own spirited, heavily syncopated Gospel rhythms. It took Mary Lee months just to learn to clap off-beat. Finally after a year, she gave up and left the music direction to someone else.

The adjustments, however, were not all on our part. Our members were also making concessions—like learning to arrive on time for services. At first it was common for folks to arrive at 8:30 for the 7:00 P.M. service. As a result the final *amen* came later and later. Finally I put my foot down.

"Service will begin at seven o'clock," I announced, "even if there's no one else here but me and my family. We will start on time."

Change came reluctantly but within a few months most people were actually arriving before seven.

Toning down some of the emotionalism was another thing. The people pounded their tambourines, danced and shouted until the last note of the organ died away. We were used to shouting in our Southern Pentecostal churches, but over the years we'd also come to value order in worship.

My first attempt at establishing discipline was to quiet the tambourines.

"How many people have your tambourines with you?"
I asked one evening. "Hold them up!"

About fifty tambourines shot up in the air.

"Now put them under your seats," I said, smiling, "and leave them there for the rest of the evening."

Miraculously it worked.

Perhaps one of the biggest adjustments for both me and my congregation came in the conduct of funerals. The day I preached my first funeral the place was packed with more curiosity seekers than mourners. It was a novelty for a white man to preach a colored funeral. Everyone wanted to see what I would do. I was pretty anxious to see what would happen myself.

Nurses were present, dressed in white uniforms and white gloves, to be with the family in case they fainted. Melancholy hymns like "Precious Memories" and "Last Mile of the Way" set the sorrowful tone.

I knew that these services had a long cultural precedent, but it was not my culture. If I attempted to preach like a black preacher, I would be parodying something I knew very little about.

While I didn't want to discourage genuine emotion, I tried to redirect it. I preached about the homecoming of the child of God, emphasizing that being absent in the body meant being present with the Lord. We shall never die. Think of it!

As I spoke quietly and joyously about resurrection, the mourners began to identify with what I was saying. Moans and tears were replaced by delighted "Amens!"

Ours became "graduating" services. I remember at one funeral an elderly man, Brother Murphy, stood for a few moments by the coffin, then reached out and clapped the deceased on his hands. "Man," he cried, "you really knocked a home run this time!"

Another time I was asked to preach a funeral for a

relative of one of our members. The service was to take place at a funeral home across town. As usual whenever I walked into a black place of business, people totally ignored me. As I entered the administrative side of the parlor the directors of the funeral home walked by me as if I were a part of the woodwork. After a few minutes I decided I'd better say something.

"Excuse me . . . could you—"

"Not now!" one man barked.

I turned to another person.

"I'm here to—"

"I'm busy," he said. "I'll see you after awhile."

So I stepped to one side, waiting until I was summoned. It wasn't long before I heard them muttering, "Where is the preacher? Why doesn't he get here?"

I decided to say nothing.

"I never heard of a Preacher Meares," one of the men I had tried to talk to said. "Who is he, anyway?"

More time passed and their annoyance grew. The chapel was full of people and it was 'way past the time announced for the service. Then one of the directors noticed me still standing in a corner.

"Who are you?" he asked.

"I'm John Meares."

His mouth dropped open.

"You've come to preach the funeral?"

"Yes," I said.

As he led me toward the chapel I struggled to stifle a grin.

Despite such animosity from strangers, from my congregation I received only support and encouragement. I was learning that when people are truly hungry for the Word of God, they don't care who feeds them. They just want that solid food.

Here was a people who hungered for God with all of

their hearts. The religious, as well as the unchurched, drank of His Spirit thirstily like people released from a season of drought. They were being set free—and I too was being set free.

The people who came to the Evangelistic Center weren't following me, they were following the Lord. I was only a guide along a portion of their journey. I had never been happier.

Mom and Dad — Sylvia and
Richie Meares.

The Bell girls in 1933: Mary
Lee, Elva, and Louise.

The Meares children in Florida. Left to right: Virgil, Paul, Velma, Maurice, and me. Bernice, my older sister, had married at the time of this picture (1935).

I fell in love with Mary Lee before I ever heard her sing. Here she is pictured on the left with the Bible School Girls Quartet in 1939.

Mary Lee and me in 1945, one year after we had said, "I do."

Starting from scratch in June of 1947, we dedicated four-and-a-half months later this lovely little church in Athens, Tenn. It was the first church we ever built (1947).

We had a daily radio program in Athens, Tenn. Pictured from left are: myself, Al Edenfield, Mary Lee, James Cooper, and Garland Mann, seated (1947).

Our family in the early days (1950). I would have never thought that my children would in later years be so closely related to me in my ministry.

Our first office staff consisted of seven people (1956).

This is the first choir, pictured in 1956.

We had a hard time finding room for all the people who were coming. Pictured here is the congregation inside the auditorium when the church was on Georgia Avenue (1964).

We were a proud congregation when we dedicated our new church building in 1975.

Vibrant John Petrucelli leading the singing.

It was a very sobering time as I was being consecrated a Bishop. Left to right: Bishop Benson Idahosa of Nigeria, Bishop Robert McAllister of Brazil, and Bishop Earl Paulk of Atlanta, Georgia, laying hands upon me (1982).

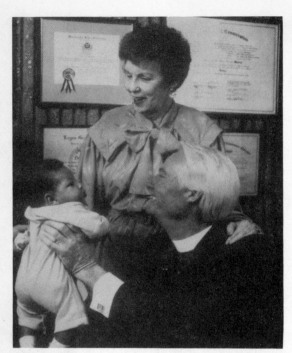

One of the joys of pastoring!

The Meares clan—celebrating our church's 30th anniversary in 1985.

12

Ministry on Trial

◆━◇ It's hard to explain denominationalism to someone who has never experienced its strengths. A person
can become so loyal to his denomination that it almost
becomes synonymous with the Kingdom of God. He
wants to see his denomination blessed, its churches grow.
If God attempts to expand him spiritually in a direction
that's unacceptable to the group, he's tempted to believe
he can't survive on his own.

I was placed in such a dilemma a year after I arrived in
Washington.

By then, church leaders were charging me with some
serious violations of denominational discipline. The
charges were multiple: disloyalty, rebellion, sowing discord among the brethren, and operating an unlicensed
ministry, among others. The first three accusations re-
sulted from my decision to assist Johnny Petrucelli's
uncle, an evangelist who was no longer a member of the
denomination, at his recent crusade in Florida.

The latter charge was directed against my ministry in Washington. The Evangelistic Center was an independent program that I had started without the approval of the denomination. I had been given twelve months to make it "acceptable."

Now church authorities summoned me to appear before a board of my peers Thursday morning, May 31, 1956, at a church in Jacksonville, Florida. In those days, starting an independent ministry was considered rebellion by the denomination. From my earliest teens I could remember hearing stories about ministers who had taken off on their own and failed miserably. They were the rebels of the faith. I didn't want to encounter the pitfalls that had ensnared them. Yet if they wanted to, I knew the church could make an example of my independence by taking my license, leaving me naked and alone.

Throughout my ministry I had tried to stand up for what I believed was right, even when it meant defending other ministers who were called on the carpet. Others had solicited my help in the past. Now I sought theirs. I spent three days calling minister friends and explaining the situation.

"Will you come to the trial and support me?" I asked.

"Sure, John," most of them replied.

I also called my family. Mama, my brother Paul, sister Velma, and cousin Wilmon Smith promised to make the five-hour drive up from Indian Rocks. The day of the trial Mary Lee and I were to move into a new house. I left her in Washington to do the moving while I went to Florida to face my judges.

It was warm in Jacksonville. A tropical breeze stirred the trees, reminding me that summer was already here. As I drove to the church from my hotel I visualized two dozen of my minister friends standing outside the church, looks of righteous indignation on their faces as they waited to be my character witnesses.

It was a terrible thing to be under the suspicion of the denomination! Church trials for ministers were secretive, closed-door sessions. Even if the charges against the accused were dropped, the taint of the trial remained around him like a stubborn odor that refused to go away.

These thoughts ran through my mind as I headed to the church. I knew that my time of avoiding serious confrontation with the church had run out. I had insisted that a court recorder (hired at my own expense) be allowed in to transcribe the hearing, and that my family be admitted into the hearing room to hear the charges against me. If my position with the church was in jeopardy, I wanted them to know why and to hear my side of the story.

Pulling up to the church, I scanned the street for cars with out-of-state license plates. There was one. My mouth felt as dry as cardboard as I walked to the basement classroom where the meeting would be held.

In the basement corridor a sinking feeling hit the pit of my stomach. Where were my friends? Waiting for me were my family and five fellow ministers, including one brother who had driven in from out-of-state. My friends explained that they had all gotten calls from church officials telling them it would be a closed trial and they would not be admitted. These brave few had decided to come anyway.

I thanked them, but inwardly I shrank from the coming session. I would be facing a board of good men, sincere men, but men extremely loyal to the traditions of our denomination.

At 11:00 A.M. I was called into the trial room. After some debate, my family was admitted inside while my friends were made to wait outside.

*   *   *

Four men sat on the board, all of them ministers and evangelists from families that were pioneers in the Pentecostal movement. Their loyalty to the denomination had earned them respect and status. The moderator of the board was a man whose ministry had led to my own conversion at age seven. I had worked with, or known, the other three over the years.

Right away I sensed I was going to be seriously reprimanded. They were going to make me an example.

Over the years I had often operated outside the strict structures of the church—though always with the consent of my own elders. After the ring incident in Athens I now allowed members of my congregation to wear wedding rings. We had used Sunday school literature other than that published by our denomination. Now I was hearing that I'd gone too far when I'd associated with an independent minister (Johnny's uncle) and started an unofficial, independent church in Washington.

"I do not have a church, I have a Revival Center," I said, using the defense that I was a missionary in Washington, not a pastor. "The difference between my program and the revivals you have in your churches is that you have one or two a year, and they terminate in two or three weeks. I have a revival every night and practically every afternoon of the year."

I explained that I had asked the church to change my status from pastor to missionary. Also, I had recently contacted my state overseer inviting him to visit and give me any advice he could about how I could bring our organization into line with church norms.

"There may be no precedent to the work we are doing," I argued, "but God is blessing mightily with souls being saved and bodies healed."

The board pondered my statement for several moments before responding with their own arguments against it.

"If every church took the view that is presented by Brother Meares," declared one district overseer, "what would become of the government of the church? If we all were to set up an independent work, where would be the centralized leadership under which we have been working and which God has been blessing through these many years?"

He was a good orator; I could see the other board members hang onto every word.

". . . In light of this sort of situation, I contend that Brother Meares' action has brought confusion—not only confusion but discord. . . ."

As the minister chastised me I knew it wasn't only my ministry, but I myself that was on trial. I loved my denomination but I had outgrown some of its concepts. In their attempt to maintain order, it seemed to me they were sacrificing the Holy Spirit's creativity. In their own way they were telling me that I had outgrown my usefulness to them as much as I had outgrown their traditional structures.

"I hope we will stand together, united, against any interdenominational movement operated by one of our preachers," the overseer continued passionately. "It will tear down the work and disturb the people of our churches."

I was hurting as it became clear how far we had grown apart from each other. I had sought God's direction in my life, but I had failed to notice His pruning. As I drew nearer to Him, I had pulled away from many of the legalisms I once accepted without question.

"Brother Meares, what do you feel the obligation of an ordained minister is to the church organization?" The question came from a minister whose grandfather had been at the forefront of the Pentecostal movement.

"If in your opinion you felt that you could do more for

God and the salvation of souls by going contrary to the set-forth practices and rules of the church," he pressed, "you would feel you had an obligation to God first? You wouldn't feel you were bound by the regulations and methods of the church?"

I knew I had to answer honestly and from my heart.

"As far as I'm concerned there is only one answer," I said. "If I thought God was speaking something different to me than to the church to which I belong . . . then I'd have to put God first. There is no other answer to give, for any of us.

"We all have to answer first to God and then to general headquarters. But I contend that we can answer to God *and* general headquarters. That is my hope.

"I am not here to tell you that I have a perfect answer," I went on. "I am not here to try to say that I'm right. Maybe I have contracted some disease that leads me to the conclusions I've reached. I am not aware that I am sick, but maybe I am. If I am, I ask you for a diagnosis, for a cure can be found only when the disease is known. If I am sick, I ask for medication. I ask for healing. Don't cast me aside. Doctor me. Sustain life in me as long as you can. . . ." I was pleading for my life as a minister.

"The charges you've brought against me," I concluded, "have far-reaching consequences. I know that in the minds of many of the best friends I shall ever have, if I cease being an ordained minister in the church, I cease to live. Please, keep me alive."

The hearing concluded without any decision being reached. Three months later their answer came: I had been disfellowshiped from the denomination. I was no longer a minister, no longer even a member of the church I had grown up in and sought to serve.

There was only one resource left open to me—to appeal the decision to the General Overseer (the highest office of the denomination), who was also my uncle. Two weeks after I filed my appeal, I sat waiting outside his office. As my appointment time came and went, I got the impression he didn't want to see me. Was he avoiding me, too?

"Mr. Meares, he can see you now," the secretary said.

I walked into the office and smiled as I embraced my mother's brother. We exchanged a few pleasantries before I launched into the charges against me.

"Uncle Zeno, you know I don't want to be disloyal to the church. I hope I can satisfy any reasonable demand."

My uncle seemed distant as he wrestled with some unspoken problem. I stopped, waiting for him to speak.

"John, you know we can't handle the situation of an integrated church," he said. "We don't know what to do with it."

So this had been the problem all the time. A load was lifted from my shoulders as I realized that discipline was not the issue, but racism.

"So that's the real complaint," I said.

He didn't respond.

"If that's the issue, then I withdraw my appeal," I said, as the brief interview ended.

I had not come to Washington to start a black church or a white church, though a white church would have been my expectation. But to be disfellowshiped from the denomination was the last thing I ever expected.

For thirty-five years our denomination had been the focus of everything I did. But as the reality of what had happened set in, I was engulfed by an unexplainable peace. I couldn't fight their attitudes about race; that was their problem, not mine.

Under church rules, Mary Lee would have been exonerated as a true and proper Christian if she left me. Instead, saying that God had called her to share my vision, she too left the church. I was grateful that when God calls a husband and wife to a ministry, what He does in the heart of one He does in the other. Though Mary Lee had also spent her whole life in the church, she too left without bitterness.

Her parents supported us, though they didn't always understand. But they lived in the town where the denomination was headquartered and were pillars in the church there. It must have saddened them tremendously when they saw the shift in attitude toward us. Previously, whenever Mary Lee and I returned to Tennessee, church officials greeted us with open arms. Now some of them crossed the street to avoid us.

My own family was supportive, too, often rallying to my defense. I did hear, however, that one of my brothers wanted to know "why John doesn't get a real job and quit living with them niggers."

13

More Walls Tumble

◆◇ The old York Theater at 3641 Georgia Avenue ran its last movie Saturday, March 17, 1957. The next morning it reopened as Evangel (meaning "Good News") Temple, our first permanent place of worship. We'd purchased the building for $125,000 and did much of the remodeling ourselves. The site would be our home for the next eighteen years.

The year following the separation from my denomination was a time of building spiritually as well. I had always been torn between my desire to travel and preach and my need to settle down as a pastor. When I traveled now, Johnny remained behind to oversee the church in Washington. I made it a point always to return for Sunday services, unless I was overseas and couldn't be back.

Still, I didn't realize how much my frequent trips were affecting my family until my five-year-old daughter Cynthia brought it to my attention.

"Where is Daddy?" she asked her mother one day.

"He's out preaching the Gospel, honey," Mary Lee told her.

Cynthia pondered this in silence for a moment.

"Then why don't we get a *new* daddy?" she asked.

That night, as was my habit daily when on the road, I called home to check on the family. After telling Mary Lee how much I loved her and how the meetings were going, I asked, "How are the children?"

"Cynthia wants a new daddy," came the startling reply, and then the whole story.

For a while I was speechless, letting my daughter's request sink in. I felt God was talking to me through Cynthia, telling me I was not fulfilling my ministry toward my family. In my zeal to serve God I had put Him first, preaching second, my family third. Were those His priorities?

Somehow I was allowing the work of God to replace the God of the work and His direction for my life. God was reminding me, through a five-year-old, that my primary role was that of pastor and father.

"I'll close the meeting this week and come home," I told Mary Lee.

I did come home and put my tent and equipment up for sale. Too many ministers had lost their wives and children through neglect, and I didn't want to be one of them.

God provided additional confirmation that Washington was my place of ministry, when I accompanied one of our visitation teams a couple of weeks later on their rounds to visit sick people in the community.

We drove to various houses and apartment buildings in Northwest Washington praying for some people, bringing food to others. We'd been out half the day when we arrived at a small, darkly lit rowhouse. Teenagers and young children were sprawled on the floor watching television, while their grandmother lay in bed in a back room.

"Grandma, the people from the church is here," a little girl yelled as she led the way to the bedroom.

We entered the room single-file with me bringing up the rear.

"You!" the old lady cried pointing to me. "You're the man! You're the man!"

Streams of tears began rolling down her face as she repeated the phrase over and over. I was shocked, trying to figure out what I had done. At last I walked over to the bed and gently took her hand.

"What do you mean, I'm the man?" I asked. It was a few minutes before she could quiet down enough to tell us the story.

"Oh, I have prayed . . . prayed so long for someone to come and preach the Word to my people," she said. "God showed me a dream, a dream with a white man. 'This is the man I will send to the city to start a church,' He told me. You are the man I saw in the dream."

Through the rest of that day and for many weeks afterwards I heard that elderly woman's words *You are the man!* ringing in my ears. Through her God had let me know that regardless of the problems, He was still in control of my life.

Around this time I was presented with a challenge I could never have accepted if I had remained within my denomination. It came about through my old friend and mentor, David du Plessis. A beloved teacher at my Bible college, this Pentecostal pioneer from South Africa had for some reason taken a personal interest in my career from the very beginning. David had been invited to address some leaders of the World Council of Churches in Switzerland. He had addressed them the previous year, but this year could not make it. He wanted me to go in his place to talk about Pentecost as a third "religious stream"—neither Protestant nor Catholic, but distinct from both.

My last encounter with Catholics had been as a young Bible school student in rural Pennsylvania, knocking on doors, including that charitable priest's, without enticing a single person to my storefront services. Now David was asking me to address religious leaders from seventy countries, most of them Catholic.

I would be the only Pentecostal attending and I was skeptical of my qualifications. David was comfortable communicating with all these different religious groups. With his quick wit and easygoing manner he could handle any situation diplomatically.

At last he persuaded me to go—with Mary Lee's promise to come along and pray all the time I was speaking! Still, I was nervous. Having grown up in a church that questioned the spiritual depth of groups like the Methodists and the Baptists, one thing we knew beyond a shadow of a doubt—the Catholics had no spirituality at all!

But Mary Lee and I attended the conference and I preached on Pentecostalism, with special emphasis on the outpouring of the Holy Spirit at the turn of the twentieth century. I couldn't tell how they were receiving this—and to make matters worse, while I was addressing these religious leaders about present-day miracles of healing, Mary Lee got sick and remained in bed with a fever through most of the conference.

A couple of weeks after we returned home, however, I got a call from Father Killion McDonald, a Jesuit priest who had attended the conference. "John," he said, "I will be in Washington for a few days speaking at the Shrine of the Immaculate Conception. If it wouldn't be an imposition, I'd like to stay at your house and learn more about the Holy Spirit."

I nearly dropped the phone. I couldn't believe it! A priest wanting to learn from me?

The climax of his stay with us was our visit to an old-fashioned Holy Ghost camp meeting that I'd heard was going on in rural Virginia, about sixty miles from Washington. It was a traditional sawdust tabernacle—the kind I remember as a little boy. In his black clerical collar, Father McDonald drew plenty of stares. I'd wanted him to get the flavor of a genuine country camp meeting, but as people sang, danced, and spoke in tongues with joyous abandon, I wondered if I was maybe pushing his education too fast.

At one point a worshiper near us was enveloped in a cloud of sawdust as he spun around and around, praising God at the top of his lungs. With a final shout, he threw up his hands and ran into the woods as fast as he could. The priest surveyed the scene with a quiet seriousness.

"What did you think?" Mary Lee asked anxiously as we headed back toward Washington.

Father McDonald considered the question.

"I believe they are sincere," he said. "Entirely sincere."

After his experience at the camp meeting, I wondered if he would want to hear anything more about Pentecostals. Mary Lee and I were both amazed and delighted when we learned a couple years later that he had received the baptism of the Holy Spirit and had spoken in tongues.

From that time on, I started thinking differently about the Catholics, trying to become less judgmental, more open as Father McDonald had been open to diverse expressions of God.

Bible Adventureland was one of the successful programs in the early days of our church.

Simply driving through the inner-city neighborhoods, one saw hundreds, perhaps thousands of children. With few decent playgrounds available to them, the streets were their summertime escape from stifling, overcrowded apartments. Evangel Temple launched a youth outreach program. We sent fourteen buses through the four quadrants of the city to round up these street kids and bring them to church for an exciting, action-packed, two-hour Sunday school session called Bible Adventureland. Here Bible stories like Elijah praying down fire from heaven came to life through skits and dramatized readings that had the children sitting on the edges of their seats.

Word about this fun Sunday school spread like brushfire. Each week we found more and more children standing together in eager bunches waiting for the buses to take them to Bible Adventureland. I don't know who looked forward to the classes more, the children or the parents and grandparents grateful to send the youngsters to someone else's care for a few hours.

The children were special to me. Racial prejudice and the controversies of religion hadn't touched them yet, so the scar tissue covering their hearts and spirits was minimal.

Bible Adventureland mushroomed. After a year, it was necessary to rent a second theater to accommodate the hundreds of children attending. I knew that if we could help these young people develop an intimate, personal relationship with God, they could use their faith to find answers to poverty and injustice.

I wasn't blind to the substandard housing, job discrimination, and social frustration that plagued the lives of my congregation. I just felt helpless to confront it. I was a pastor, not a reformer. With my Southern background and political ignorance, any social activism that I launched would probably make matters worse, not better.

How could I encourage my parishioners to boycott a store or integrate a restaurant? I had no political savvy. My faith was in the Gospel, not social protest. I knew that God's Word transformed people, and people transformed circumstances.

Maybe my feelings were a cop-out, but I honestly didn't believe I had yet gained enough acceptance to agitate for political change. There was much the church could do, though. We could build the children a place to play, a summer camp—Camp Adventureland.

I had seen them throughout Maryland and Virginia— rustic, well-equipped youth camps offering all the activities young people enjoy. Brother Tippett, an elderly white man who attended Evangel Temple for several years, had just died leaving us assets worth $80,000.

With the approval of the congregation I purchased 248 acres of lush wooded countryside in Culpeper, Virginia, seventy miles from Washington. The camp project quickly caught the imagination of our people. For two years they poured funds into the building program. Those unable to give financially volunteered their free time to clear trees, dig trails, and build cabins. Others set up a fund to send needy children to the camp without charge.

Phase I of the building plan completed, Camp Adventureland opened with a five-acre manmade lake for fishing and swimming; horseback riding trails; a softball diamond; an outdoor amphitheater where plays like "David and Goliath" were presented at night under the stars; cabins for 150 kids; and a dining hall that doubled as an activities center. Many of the older teenagers from church served as volunteer camp counselors.

We had a wonderful time that first summer. At least a thousand children spent a week in the clear fresh air. At the end of the summer, the whole church held a family picnic at Camp Adventureland.

Our peace, however, was short-lived. In 1959, Virginia remained a bastion of the old South. That year public school officials in a county near the camp closed down the entire system rather than follow a federal court mandate to desegregate. The school doors remained closed five years, shutting out more than four thousand black and white students.

The second summer we opened, I began getting reports that state troopers were harassing our children whenever they ventured off camp property to walk into town. Also, Phase II of our building program was being held up by county zoning and building officials who refused every plan we submitted.

I had visited several nearby camps in search of models. Using some of their ideas along with my own, I had determined that our camp would rival any other in the state. Still our plans and permits were refused. I knew that our design wasn't the problem. The problem was our people.

In those days most of the people attending Evangel Temple were just working-class poor folks. Day laborers, government office-cleaners, chauffeurs, and domestics who spent their days serving others. I knew they had dreams and aspirations of their own—many that would never be fulfilled—but to most of the white people who hired them, they were just that—hired help. Not people at all.

Over the years I had observed Washington's racism, and by being quiet participated in it. Time had taught me that there were two kinds of racism—the hate-activated kind such as we were encountering in rural Virginia, and the benign neglect of people like myself who never confronted the problem because they "didn't know what to do." God would take care of the situation. Gradually I realized He was trying to take care of it—through me!

Every Christian must know his calling and his limits. By nature I am not a confrontational person; that was my limit. But I also knew God had called me to a ministry whose very character created confrontation. How I was to resolve this tension I didn't know. But for now I knew I had to fight.

In building Camp Adventureland I had begun to identify with the struggles and frustrations of my people. We had been complying with the law, intending to build according to code, but it seemed there was no law or code for us. With each attempt to fit in, the laws and codes were changed to ensure that we wouldn't.

Now we adjusted our plans yet again and I took them back to the county building official. This time, however, I was prepared for the resistance.

As I had expected, the plans were not approved. But this time I questioned every argument raised and presented proof of our compliance. As I challenged the official, I could see his anger mounting steadily, heating up his complexion till he appeared about to explode. He finally did.

"Preacher," he said, and added some less flattering forms of address, "you can keep this up if you want. But I warn you, we're going to run you and them niggers out of here!"

At least it was finally out in the open. I walked to the door of his office and turned to respond before leaving.

"You won't run me out of here," I said quietly. "We'll be here long after you're gone."

During those days, the government of the District of Columbia was run by commissioners appointed by Congress. Johnny Petrucelli got an appointment with the elderly Southern senator who oversaw the activities of the commission to ask if he could use his influence in helping us get the camp completed.

"Sir, we need this camp," Johnny explained. "I work with youth in this community and I see the growing militancy they're exposed to. Radical groups are encouraging children to vent their frustrations through violence. I'm afraid that if something isn't done to relieve the pressure, one day the violence that has rocked other parts of this country will hit Washington, D.C. Maybe it won't be as bad if we try to provide healthy outlets."

As Johnny spoke the old senator crossed his legs on his desk and looked at Johnny with a sarcastic grin.

"Son, where did you say your pastor was from?" he asked.

"Tennessee, sir."

"And I detect a Southern accent from you. You're from the South, too?"

"Yes, sir."

"Then I would suggest that you and your pastor go back to the cotton fields as soon as possible. Evidently you don't belong here. Do you know how big this city's police force is?" His voice was rising with anger. "Are you aware of the military personnel stationed at Andrews Air Force Base, Fort Myers, Fort Meade? We've got FBI headquarters here, and the CIA—thousands of law enforcement personnel! There will never be any violence in this city. It'll never happen here, son. So I suggest that you and your pastor hurry back to Tennessee. Good day."

Political pressure hadn't worked—or we were inept at it. But prayer did. Camp Adventureland remained a respite from steamy summer pavements, even growing larger over the years.

14 ◆━◇━◆━◇━◆━◇━◆━◇━◆

"You Are My Pastor"

◆◇ "Pastor, are you ready for a shocker?" asked Johnny.

George Smith* was a gifted black evangelist and singer who was extremely popular with the people at the church. He had been introduced to us by a minister friend who had heard him speak at a church conference.

Since we were always on the lookout for good evangelists, black or white, we had enthusiastically sponsored George and made him part of our church family. In the past four years, our relationship had grown ever stronger. Or so I had thought, until Johnny called me while I was on one of my now-infrequent trips overseas with Mary Lee.

"George came to see me before service today," Johnny continued, "and told me the Lord said we're supposed to give him everything we collect for tithes and offerings this week. What do you want me to do?"

---

* Not his real name.

George had often told me that we paid him better than anywhere else he went. Although I believed this preacher was a man of God, I couldn't believe that the Lord wanted us to overlook our obligations to our creditors and our small church staff.

"Johnny, you're in charge," I said, "so you'll have to judge. If that's what you think you should do, okay. However, I personally have a very difficult time accepting that the Lord wants us to give George our whole income for the week. There are a lot of other people we are responsible to."

Three days later Mary Lee and I returned home and learned the end of the story that very evening from Johnny. He hadn't given George all the tithes and offerings. That night at the Sunday evening service, George was scheduled to sing and preach. The church was packed with members and visitors.

It was a joyous atmosphere with the choir singing, the audience clapping. At one point George picked up a microphone and began singing "Oh Happy Day," his signature song. With his strong baritone booming throughout the church it wasn't long before he had everyone swaying and moving to the song with him. Then he began to speak.

"The Holy Spirit is a liberating Spirit."

"Yes!" the crowd had responded.

"He's here tonight to free you!"

"Hallelujah!"

George went on to observe that black people had never been free in America.

"We've been field slaves and kitchen slaves. Whether it's working in the fields of the government or the kitchens of the church, we need to be free!"

By now Johnny sensed something was wrong.

"Aren't you tired of being a kitchen slave?" George shouted.

"Yes!"

"Isn't it time you got out of the fields of slavery?"

"Yes, Lord!"

"But here you are, still serving the slavemasters!" he cried, pointing to Johnny.

"The masters have big homes, nice cars, lots of money. The slaves remain in the kitchen and the fields. You might have a white pastor, but he's got a black heart. If you want to be freed from slavery tonight, stand up!"

Within an instant two or three hundred people were on their feet. George walked off the platform and headed for the back of the church. "All of you who want to be delivered, follow me!" he called, walking down the aisle and out the door, followed by most of those who were standing.

Johnny, meanwhile, had stepped into the pulpit. "Now if everyone has left who so desires, we will continue the service." He turned to the choir, had them sing a couple of songs, tried to say a few comforting remarks to the remaining people, then dismissed them.

"Pastor, I just let them go," Johnny said, winding up the story. "I did what I could—I just didn't know what to do."

For a few minutes we sat in silence, letting the significance of what had happened seep into our spirits. It had finally happened. The unrest, the undercurrent of racial hostility that we'd felt but had never confronted, had been used as a wedge to split the church.

Mary Lee sighed and turned to me.

"Thank God. For the first time someone's said it openly, rather than behind our backs," she said.

The next morning I set out on one of the hardest missions since coming to Washington. I had prayed most of the night, asking God what I should do. The answer came just after dawn: *Go see George Smith and ask him to come back to the church. Forgive him.*

We'd rented an apartment at the Cavalier Hotel on 14th Street to house visiting evangelists and George was staying there. Walking into the building, I encountered a line of people that stretched across the lobby. They were all members—or, I supposed, former members—of my church waiting to see George for spiritual counseling. I overheard one group talking about the church he planned to start in Washington.

Locating a lady who seemed to be in charge, I asked to see George. She pointed me to a corner and told me to wait. For the next hour I sat alone waiting as Evangel Temple regulars walked by without speaking or looking in my direction. I had become an invisible man.

The humiliation and isolation were almost more than I could bear. But because God had told me to talk to George, I continued to wait. When it became clear that I wasn't leaving, George sent a message that he didn't want to talk to me. I left without arguing, wondering, *Lord, what am I supposed to do now?*

For the remainder of that week I prayed. Was this the end of my ministry here in Washington? Would the remaining members leave, too? Had I failed to recognize the gulf that had come between us?

Sunday morning arrived without any answers or revelations. It was as if God had joined the offended faction of the church. He too was ignoring me.

When I arrived at church that morning, the sanctuary was packed, with extra chairs lining the aisles and people standing in the back. Word had gotten out about what had happened and everyone was curious to see what I had to say. No one was more curious than I was.

Service started with singing, then Johnny led the congregation in prayer. Next I was supposed to read my text and preach. I stood up and a deathly hush fell over the church. No one moved or stirred. The silence was so heavy it magnified every little sound in the building.

All eyes were fixed on me as I walked down the steps from the speaker's platform onto the main floor. I remained silent, still unsure of what to say or do. I had never walked out into the congregation before and didn't know why I was doing so now. People seemed mesmerized as I began a slow trek down the center aisle, carefully placing one foot in front of the other.

All was silent except for the dull tread of my footsteps. I was halfway to the rear when she grabbed me—a big, husky woman with tears streaming down her face. She pulled me to her bosom and began rocking me in her arms.

"You are my pastor, you are my pastor," she cried between sobs. "You are my pastor."

Over and over she repeated the words. Slackening her hold on me, she turned to face the congregation.

"We've never declared this man as our pastor," she said. "It's time we made a formal declaration as a church."

Escorting me to the front of the sanctuary, she turned me to face the congregation. I remained speechless, unable to say a word.

Looking over the crowd she asked, "Are you ready to let this man know he's our pastor?"

Silence. Then a woman slipped out of the first row, walked up to me, and hugged me.

"You are my pastor," she said softly.

Another followed, repeating the ritual. One by one, the women left their seats and joined the line to hug me and declare, "You are my pastor."

Everyone sat transfixed throughout the strange ceremony. When all of the women had come forward, one of the men stood up and asked, "What are we men gonna do? Are we gonna declare that this man's our pastor?"

One by one the men came. As each one embraced me he announced, "You are my pastor."

It was a wondrous moment. God in His own manner and timing had demonstrated our unity. If I had asked for the congregation's support I'm not sure what would have happened, even though I believed that they loved me.

Later that morning when I turned to my Bible for a text to preach from, I opened to a Scripture I had long since forgotten.

"And hath made of one blood all nations of men for to dwell on all the face of the earth" (Acts 17:26, KJV).

Within a few weeks all but six of the members who had walked out with George Smith returned to Evangel Temple.

15

Drenched in the Latter Rain

◆◇ During the '60s we faced the growing pains of social change and self-discovery along with the rest of the nation. As the pastor of a black inner-city church (the terms *colored* and *Negro* were now gone as a result of the black pride movement), it was impossible for me not to be affected by the turmoil of the civil rights era.

In 1963, the capital became the focal point of the civil rights movement with the historic March on Washington. Dr. Martin Luther King, Jr., the black Southern minister whose leadership had served as the catalyst for the movement, mobilized hundreds of thousands of people across the country, white and black, poor and rich, political and apolitical, in one of the largest demonstrations of unity in the history of our nation. As I watched the marchers converge on the Washington Mall, I was mesmerized by their kinship. Like one big family, they walked arm-in-arm in a multi-ethnic sea of humanity that covered the area around the Reflecting Pool and stretched away as far as you could see.

I had come to the Mall with a group of clergy. As the old Gospel hymn "We Shall Overcome"—the anthem of the movement—emerged from somewhere deep within the marchers we joined the rumble of voices, rising and swelling into a thunderous crescendo of sound.

When Dr. King's resonant baritone rang out the stirring words "I have a dream," I could see that dream in my spirit and identify with it. Like Dr. King, I was involved in a spiritual revival. Despite the political overtones of the civil rights movement, I began to see that it was really a God-ordained struggle based not so much on the Constitution as on the Bible. Until all people, black and white, were free of their insecurities, false superiority, and hatreds, we could not leave the ancestral dwelling places of our souls to journey to a new place to worship God.

With new times, Evangel Temple got an influx of new people. Along with the faithful old-timers—the charter members whose loyalty formed the backbone of the ministry—there was an influx of people like Robert Matthews, street-wise and street-tough young Washingtonians whose outspokenness and drive stood in sharp contrast to the quiet reserve of many of the older members.

A native Washingtonian and the eighth of ten children, Robert Matthews was a scrapper and a survivor. He was bright and energetic, but like most of the guys in his neighborhood devoid of purpose. The prevailing attitude of most young men like him was, If you are black, why bother? Neither education nor talent got you any farther than the system allowed you to go.

Robert worked as a stock clerk at a local department

store. His real livelihood, however, came from his avocation as a professional gambler. In two or three days of gambling, he could make twice his monthly salary earned stacking boxes, and also command the respect of his neighborhood. In the vernacular of the streets, Robert at age twenty was "cool" and in control. Amazingly, and without forethought, he suddenly relinquished that control to God at one of our revival meetings.

Five of his brothers and sisters had been attending the church for the past couple of years. Fearing that the streets would get Robert before God did, they had been relentless in their witnessing to him. But Robert remained aloof and unimpressed until his sister Claudean tried a novel approach.

"Robert, why don't you go to church to just let the Lord know you know about Him?" she suggested.

For some reason this appealed to him. With this intention in mind, he came to a revival service with another sister, Dorothy. Before the night was over they were both hooked on the church and God.

After that, whenever the church doors opened Robert was there. Within three years he was traveling as an evangelist, preaching his way across the United States before returning to Evangel Temple to serve as a youth leader, usher, altar counselor, and Bible teacher. Eventually he became the first elder ordained by Evangel Temple.

About this time I was undergoing a major transformation in my ministry, partly as a result of the influence of the apostle Nicholas Bengu.

Nicholas Bengu was a black South African minister who was regarded by his own people—and by many whites—as South Africa's Billy Graham. In a country torn apart by racial hatred, Brother Bengu was an apostle of unity. The descendant of Zulu royalty, Brother Bengu had embraced Marxism early in his life, later converted to Christianity. Wherever he preached the Gospel, his words had a transforming effect. Some people were healed physically. Others experienced spiritual renewal, dedicating or rededicating their lives to Jesus Christ. Above all, this twentieth-century apostle and his people demonstrated a unity of spirit and purpose that I greatly desired. Evangel Temple in comparison was disjointed. Even though there were overflow crowds and healings of every description, I detected a lack of commitment and cohesion. Yes, we had the best evangelists coming in, the crowds were there, souls being saved, but it seemed that it was a turnover crowd. The back door was as big as the front.

People would tell me what wonderful sermons I was preaching. If so, why was I feeling so dry in my spirit? Why were our people not being established? I needed a fresh word from God.

The Cavalier Apartment Hotel was nearby. I rented a room and let only my wife and a couple of others know where I would be, in case of emergency.

The Holy Spirit was leading me on a forty-day fast. It was all happening within my mind, but the pictures were clear and sharp. Scenes from my life appeared before me like slides flashing across a screen. Growing up in Indian Rocks, Florida. Bible school in Tennessee. The early years of marriage. The churches in Athens and Memphis. The move to Washington.

I was reminded of some of the miracles I'd experienced personally. Mary Lee and me praying for our three-year-old Donnie the day I backed the car over him in our driveway. An hour later he was back playing, the black treadmark burns still visible on his body.

Or the time I'd been returning home from Evangel Temple, windows rolled down because of the summer heat. As I'd waited at a red light, a young man in his teens stepped in front of my car. The light turned green and I tapped the horn for him to move, but he didn't.

At that moment I felt an arm coming through the driver's window and going around my neck. "Give me your wallet!" I did so. But then the passenger door opened and another teenager got into the car with a gun pointed at me.

In an instant my fear turned to supernatural boldness. I said, "In the name of Jesus, put that gun down and get out of my car." The fellow looked bewildered. I said, "You heard me. In the name of Jesus put down that gun and get out of this car." He said, "Man, I ain't never heard anybody talk like that." And to my amazement he obeyed.

About a block away the guy who had taken my wallet was coolly looking through it. I got out of the car and yelled to him, "In the name of Jesus, you bring me back my wallet and every credit card in it." This time I wasn't surprised when he did as I said. When he got a few feet from me he threw the billfold down. The credit cards spilled over the pavement. I stooped down, picked each of them up, and got back into my car. It was only as I was nearing my house that I realized the power I'd witnessed in the name of Jesus.

I recalled the time we'd pulled James Massie from the bottom of our swimming pool. Brother Massie was a three-hundred-pound man who'd driven a busload of thirty kids out to the house for a swim party. One of the kids had rushed into the kitchen to tell Mary Lee, "There's a man in the bottom of the pool." I ran outside, dove into the pool, and with the boys' help got Brother Massie onto the pavement. I began giving resuscitation and praying. He lay lifeless, water pouring from his mouth. Then I heard a groan that was music to my ears. By the time the paramedics arrived he was semiconscious, repeating over and over, "Get right with God, boys. Get right with God." At the hospital the attending physicians said it was impossible for a person to have that much water in his lungs and live.

These scenes came back to me as powerful reminders that God was directing and ordering my life. Each day as I fasted, God made the issues clearer to me. He showed me that my congregation knew Him primarily through the ministries of the prominent healing evangelists we had hosted. We had made healing the focal point of our services.

True, these men were performing God's work, and had blessed us greatly over the years. But it was time for our people to mature, to be established in His Word. To be a blessing, not just come to receive blessings.

Forty days later I left that hotel renewed in faith and recommitted to a new direction. I began my ministry anew, initiating a strong teaching program. For two years I read my Bible night and day. It seemed to be a new Book. Evangel offered classes on everything: Communion, covenant relationships, faith, prophecy, worship, discipline, and baptism. As we strove to lay new foundation stones, the emphasis of the ministry changed from one that stressed God's blessing for the believer, to one that called on the believer to serve as a priest, blessing God.

At first most people seemed confused by the new teachings. Some accepted them reluctantly; others, including Johnny Petrucelli, could not. Mary Lee, who had always stood with me, was confused, too, and asked a lot of questions.

"John, I don't understand. If what you have found is so great, why are all these people leaving?"

I didn't know myself; I only knew I was doing what God told me I must. In the Bethesda Missionary Temple in Detroit was a congregation worshiping God the way I believed He wanted to be worshiped. This great church was pastored by Mrs. M. D. Beall and her son Jim.

I drew encouragement from their example—and I needed encouragement. People were quitting Evangel Temple now in hundreds. We'd opened a floodgate, all right, but instead of people flowing in, they flowed out, turned off by our "overemphasis" on praise. We had stopped singing many of the old gospel hymns, and were teaching the people psalms and spiritual choruses instead. We opened each service by standing and praising God for as long as half-an-hour. Believers were encouraged to desire and to develop their gifts of prophecy.

As word of these changes spread across the country, I started getting calls from minister friends. "What's happened to you, John?"

Long-time Pentecostal associates began pulling away from me. Even my mentor, David du Plessis, flew to Washington in alarm. "John, what's this I hear about you?" After we'd talked for several hours, he said, "That's exactly what I believe. Now I can fly back home."

The heaviest blow, to me, was losing Johnny. He explained that he wanted to be involved in overseas missions. Friends were supposedly helping him establish an economic base for such a program. He offered few details and I didn't press for any. All I knew was that he was leaving Evangel Temple.

I was crushed, heartbroken. Somehow I had believed Johnny and I would be together forever. Reluctantly I announced his plans to the congregation and we held a going-away service for his family. It was a joyful, somber event, with people crying and wishing him well.

For weeks afterwards I was depressed, grieving over the departure of my associate. One morning I was sitting at the breakfast table, batting back tears, when Sister Avis, our housekeeper, decided she had had it.

"Enough!" she exclaimed, throwing up her hands. "This has gone on too long."

She then soundly rebuked me, reminding me how David had nearly grieved his kingdom into despair after losing his son Absalom. "It's time to let go," she said.

Her rebuke resounded in my spirit and from that moment began my recovery.

Shortly afterward I was cheered when our son Virgil, who'd attended both Oral Roberts University and my former Bible college, joined Evangel's staff as my associate pastor.

16

In Clouds of Smoke

◆◇ The day Martin Luther King, Jr. died, I stood on the roof of the Hyatt Regency Hotel in Rosslyn, Virginia, watching the dream of racial harmony go up in clouds of billowing black smoke. Washington was burning. Riots had broken out in poor black neighborhoods after the media reported the slaying. Along the 14th Street Corridor, bands of angry mobs roamed the streets, looting businesses and burning them to the ground.

I'd been attending a ministers' conference at the hotel when I heard the news. I raced to the top of the building to watch the city burning across the Potomac River.

I was numbed by the horror of Dr. King's death. A few months before I'd gone to hear Dr. King speak at a church in the Anacostia area of Washington. He'd addressed 750 black pastors on their responsibility to the church. As far as I could see, I was the only white person present. Even then, Dr. King had spoken of his death as if he had a premonition of it. Now he was gone, silenced by the hatred he had tried to fight with peace.

I drove back into the District praying that our church hadn't been torched or any of our members hurt. Police barricades had been erected in strategic spots throughout the downtown area to keep the bulk of the looters corralled inside the 14th Street Corridor. It looked as if we were at war. Evangel Temple was located behind enemy lines and I was caught outside. Unable to continue up 14th Street, I headed home.

It was 1968, seven years since the senator had laughed Johnny to scorn, telling him there was no way blacks would ever have the courage to riot in Washington.

I reached home to find Mary Lee on the phone in the kitchen. As soon as she'd hang up, it would ring again. "John, thank God you're home!" she said, catching sight of me. "Church members have been calling all day, warning us not to go out."

"Is anyone at the church?" I asked.

"I don't know," she replied. "I don't know who's been able to get there."

We wouldn't find out what had happened at the church until the next morning.

The entire area of the city had been blighted. The only reminder of the furniture store across the street from the church was an empty storefront window littered with shards of shattered glass. Next to it firebombs burned the People's Drugstore beyond repair, sending flames shooting up into the apartments above the store and into the adjoining buildings. A church member, Ersmine Riley, lost everything in her apartment above the drugstore.

In one night, almost everything in Evangel Temple's vicinity had disappeared. But the church was still standing, thanks to the courage of a middle-aged woman named Minnie White.

"Dr. King's been shot!" a man exclaimed, running into the Helping Hand station. "People are going crazy!"

The Helping Hand was our food and clothing distribution center for the needy, located around the corner from the church.

"Oh no, I know they're going to try to torch the church," Minnie told her co-worker. "We got to save it."

With that, Minnie picked up her purse, closed shop, and marched around the corner to pray and wait. By the time the first mob hit the block where the church was located, she stood there, a lone sentry, praying and determined.

"Get out of the way, Sister. We're gonna burn this church down," a man yelled, rearing back to throw a firebomb.

"No, you ain't! Put that thing down!" Minnie commanded.

The man paused, puzzled. "This is a white preacher's church."

"This is God's church," Minnie retorted, "and you ain't gonna burn it."

Back and forth they wrangled until the mob walked away in disgust as Minnie stood there praising the Lord. All around her rioters continued to burn and loot while Minnie stood her ground.

Thus we survived the worst of the riots, escaping the destruction that came to other churches in the city, all because of God's grace expressed through one little saint. But by no means was our battle over. It was just beginning.

"Reverend Meares, good morning."

I recognized the voice, a police lieutenant from the Second District station that covered our area.

"Reverend Meares, we've heard through the grapevine that your church is going to have some unwanted visitors this morning. I'm calling to see what you want us to do about it."

For a moment I tensed. I knew exactly what he was talking about. For several months now, various churches in the city had been the target of a militant protest group known as the "Black Front." This band of dashiki-clad men and women was attempting to exact funds and property from white and black churches alike as "payment" for their negligence of the poor—though everyone doubted that the poor saw any of the money thus collected.

It was rumored that a number of church councils had voted to set aside extortion funds to keep the group from hitting their churches. Now apparently it was our turn.

"Thank you, Lieutenant. I appreciate your call. With God's help I think we can take care of them on the inside of the church. When we get them outside, it's in your hands."

"All right, Reverend," he sighed. "I'll put a car on patrol around your church just to keep an eye on you."

That Sunday morning we were concluding a week-long youth conference attended by teenagers from churches across the country. The church was full with more young folks than we'd seen in a long time. The music director was leading the congregational singing and I was on my way to the sanctuary from Sunday school next door, when I was almost run over by Mae Gunn on her way out of the church.

"Here's my tithes, Pastor," she said, stuffing an envelope into my hand.

"Mae, what's wrong?"

"You see those people across the street?" she asked. I turned to look. About two dozen men, along with several women, wearing African clothing and carrying canes, stood across the street watching us.

"There's going to be trouble at church," said Mae, "and I'm leaving."

I entered the sanctuary and took my place with the others on the platform as the congregation moved into worship. We had now come to know much more about "true worship." It was powerful! Eyes closed and arms raised, hundreds of men and women lifted melodic voices in praise of God. The joyful sound filled the sanctuary as the thirty or so members of the Black Front I had seen outside came marching down the aisles waving their canes and shouting slogans. Their shouts were drowned out by the unison worship. No one but a couple of ushers, whom they shoved aside, even knew a protest was occurring, until the group reached the front of the church.

I stood up slowly, straining as if I were pushing a heavy weight off me.

"Men, you must respect the house of God," I told them.

"White man, we want to speak," a spokesman said, starting to mount the platform.

I could feel the tension behind me as the people on the platform shifted in their seats. *Keep calm*, I said to myself.

"We're here to worship God," I said. "You can't get up here to speak."

"No, man, we're gonna talk," he said.

"You must respect the house of God," I repeated, "or we will have to usher you out."

It was as if I'd thrown gasoline on a fire. The whole group surged forward, all talking at once. It was time to act. We were in church. They were disrupting our service. Unsure of what would happen, I looked out over the congregation and commanded, "Every man stand to your feet!"

To my great comfort, every man—young and old, black and white—rose like a trained choir. Nobody was more surprised by this than me, but I kept my expression as placid as possible as I looked down at the Black Front.

"One more time, you cannot stay in this church and show disrespect for God," I said. "You may worship with us or you may leave."

Again they clamored to take the platform.

"Men, come forward," I called.

They moved from every direction—from behind me, from the rear of the sanctuary, from the pews—marching to the front of the church like a disciplined army.

Pointing to the intruders, I instructed, "Men, in the name of Jesus, put them out!"

At that point the scene took on a free-for-all aspect as the women began praising the Lord and the men throwing punches as they wrestled the protesters toward the door.

"Hey, man, we're soul brothers!" one shouted as Elder Robert pushed him along. "Soul brothers!" Some were carried out bodily, feet first. A couple of guys threw punches at Virgil and Donnie and gasped in surprise as my sons promptly returned them. Walking toward the door, I saw Sister Martha Hillard, a large woman in her sixties, standing in the aisle, one upraised hand praising the Lord, the other beating a protester over the head with her umbrella.

The police lieutenant, meanwhile, had kept his promise. As the men were carrying our unwanted guests out crying, "In the name of Jesus!" the police were waiting with a paddy wagon to grab them. In the scuffle one of the guys spit in my face and another caught me on the temple with a screwdriver. Despite the warm blood trickling down the side of my face I felt victorious. We were a people! We'd stood together against those who would divide us. Realizing that only our unity had made us strong, we returned to the sanctuary to worship as never before.

After the service, several men came to me privately to talk.

"Pastor, before this happened I didn't know what I would do in a situation like that. Now I know. I'm a Christian! Not white or black, just a Christian."

I believe we were the first church to challenge the Black Front. I heard that after their visit to Evangel Temple, they took bullhorns to their protests to ensure they would be heard above the worship. They never came back to our church, but our troubles with them were far from over.

As for the teenagers attending the youth week, for months afterwards we got letters from young people telling us that ours was the most exciting conference they'd ever attended. . . .

When we joined the city in pressing charges against the Black Front, Temple member Ed Lawson warned me to expect retaliation. Formerly in the Black Front himself, he had been saved and now belonged to our church. He appointed himself my bodyguard.

At the arraignment hearing, I got a taste of what was ahead.

A female member of the organization had gone to the district attorney charging that I had beaten her baby before the congregation. She came to court carrying a pitiful little two-year-old whose body was covered with bruises.

"He beat my baby," she told the judge. "That white man gets up in front of that church and declares he can make those niggers do anything he wants them to!"

The accusation was too outrageous to respond to.

131

"Judge," I said, "I'm here because I want this city to stand up and protect its citizens. If this group has the right to burst into a church, put fear in people's hearts and disrupt services, then we're living in a jungle."

"He's lying!" one of the accused shouted. "We didn't disrupt nothing."

Our greatest asset was Ed Lawson's testimony. He was able to identify many of the intruders by name and give inside information about their activities.

As the hearings continued, so did the threats against our lives. I received telephone calls regularly threatening me and my family. The final straw came the night a convertible full of black men carrying shotguns circled the church waiting for us to come out from evening service. It was one thing to endanger my own life but another matter to involve Mary Lee and the kids. I called a family council.

Without trying to sound too alarming, I talked about the phone calls and how our lives could be in danger if the tensions between us and the Black Front continued.

"It would be very easy for those guys to find out where we live," I said. "It's not enough to make up my own mind. I need to know how you feel."

Three teenagers listened intently. Cynthia, the youngest, was only 14 at the time and always the shy one. Now she was the first to speak up.

"Dad, didn't you say the Lord sent you here?" she asked.

I nodded yes.

"Then it's up to Him to take care of us. I'm not afraid. I say let's keep on."

One by one Mary Lee, Cynthia, Virgil, and Donnie expressed their confidence in God. Whatever happened we would not back away from the court confrontation.

When it became apparent that we weren't running

scared, the threats slacked off. The court case ended with the protesters being fined a hundred dollars for disturbing the peace.

With changes in the law, District residents eventually got the chance to elect their own city council. Some of the city's leading street activists traded in their dashikis for pin-striped suits and a role in the political process.

I saw the leader of the Black Front many years later at a Methodist minister's retirement ceremony being held in the dining hall of our new church. He was seated on the dais a few seats away, studiously not looking in my direction. When the dinner concluded, I pushed my way through the crowd and threw my arms around him.

"How are you?" I asked. "Do you remember me?"

"Yes," he said, pulling away from my embrace.

"I just wanted to thank you," I went on. "You remember the day you led the Black Front into our church over on Georgia Avenue? Well, that was the day you made us a united people! Thanks."

17

Arise and Build

◆◇ We were a united people, but by 1971 we were a very small one. Our era as an integrated church had gone up in the smoke of the burning city, in the riots of 1968. Before then, close to one-third of the eight hundred to a thousand who attended Evangel Temple regularly were white District residents, or white suburbanites who drove in for the services. That changed almost overnight as white faces disappeared like snow melting under the heat of racial violence. Suddenly we were an all-black congregation. And an increasingly black city, as the fear of continued violence drove hundreds of white District residents out of the inner city into the suburbs.

This population shift, plus the unpopularity of our emphasis on teaching and worship, had reduced our congregation to between 250 to 300 people. No new folks were coming in. I think we would have almost been embarrassed if visitors had come. Two-thirds of the church auditorium was roped off so we wouldn't be so scattered. It was as if we were marooned on a desert island, quarantined from the rest of the city.

So none of us could believe it when prophecy began coming forth from all over this small congregation to "arise and build."

With so few people, could God possibly be telling us we needed more space? We weren't beginning to fill the building we were in.

But the same astonishing word kept coming. We already owned a large lot in Edgewood—a run-down black neighborhood in Northeast Washington. Not much was in the area except dilapidated warehouses and railroad sheds. But we knew a Metro stop was going to be coming just a block away, which would give us good transportation and revitalize the area. We saw the lot as a place to plant a church that would rise as a garden in the ghetto. But could it be done?

We were a church comprised of singles, young families, retirees, and blue-collar workers—no professionals or business people among us. How could such a group launch a multi-million dollar building project? The one thing we had going for us was that we were united in believing God had said, "Arise and build."

The garden in the ghetto theme began to permeate my sermons. It was in my mind as I helped draw up the plans for the building—designing an open, airy sanctuary with cathedral roofing inset with cylinder lights that dotted the ceiling like stars. A huge royal blue backdrop behind the pulpit and choir would rise to the ceiling like an expanse of summer sky. The building would be the soil where believers would be planted in the Word. Their spirits would spring open like flowers as they grew in grace in our beautiful garden.

Everyone began asking God to help him give—even if it meant taking out a loan to do so. Young teenagers would say, "I want to give a thousand dollars." Some of them gave the money they had saved up to go to college. And to my knowledge not one of them lacked the money for school when it came time to go! God provided as only He can.

Reminiscent of Memphis and the "church that was built by night," in the evenings and on weekends volunteer crews did the work we didn't have to contract out. Both our sons worked long hours, learning to do things they had never done before. The women brought baskets of food for the volunteer help. Everyone was pitching in.

Like Gideon's three hundred, the people of Evangel Temple had accepted a challenge that "in the natural" was impossible. Some were turned down for loans by banks and credit unions. Others earned so little money or were already so deep in debt that even if they did succeed in borrowing money I feared they'd have difficulty paying it back. Just as I'd been sure Nora Crittenden in Athens couldn't pay her tithes, and blind Aunt Mary didn't have fifty cents to give away to the church, I felt they couldn't "afford" to pledge to the building fund. But God requires not our gifts but our obedience. When we follow the Word He has spoken to us, as with Abraham, He provides the abundance.

Elder Robert Matthews was among the first to borrow a thousand dollars. His father, who was not a member, thought he was crazy. "You're letting them take advantage of you," his father said. "That white preacher is brainwashing you." But neither Robert nor the others gave in to ridicule. One by one they returned with their pledges in their hands—and their testimonies as to how God had provided.

James Randolph tried borrowing at several banks with no success. The only other thing he knew to do was ask his boss where he worked for a loan. James had worked

for his company many years as a concrete-laying super-
intendent. He prayed for the Lord to give him courage and
favor when he went in to see his employer.

But the first time he asked the secretary to see his boss
she told him, "I'm sorry, he's out of town and won't be
back until next week."

When next week came he walked into the office again
and said, "I'd like to see Mr. Keel."

"Oh, I'm sorry, you just missed him."

The next day the same thing happened. This was
strange. Mr. Keel was always around; James usually saw
him every day. Now he had tried three times to see him
and failed.

"I'll try one more time and that's it," he decided. It was
just before Christmas, when his boss usually gave him a
bonus of a hundred dollars. He would donate that to the
building fund, and hope to raise some more some other
way.

Around ten o'clock the next morning he again walked
into Mr. Keel's office, thinking, *Surely he'll be in today.*
But no, once again the secretary said, "Mr. Keel had some
business to take care of today, but he did leave this
envelope for me to give you."

Disappointed, James took the envelope—it must contain his hundred-dollar bonus—and put it into his shirt
pocket. Later as James was eating lunch he remembered
the envelope. He reached into his shirt pocket, took it out,
and opened it. He couldn't believe his eyes. This year's
bonus check was for $4,000! Elated, he gave $2,000 to the
building fund.

Elder Robert, whose father had been so disgusted, paid
back his thousand-dollar loan and also fulfilled a promise
to his family that he would buy them a house. To do so he
worked full-time at the Commerce Department, then
drove a cab at night and on Saturdays. He earned nearly

enough money from the cab to support his family and used his government salary to put a hefty payment down on a house. Within a year of his pledge the Matthews family had their new house and Robert had jumped three grades on his Commerce job.

One of the most unusual testimonies came from Louise Baker, a domestic in her sixties. Week by week Sister Baker had contributed throughout the three years of the building fund. One day she came up to Mary Lee and handed her an envelope with $135.05 in it.

"This," she said with a triumphant smile, "completes my pledge to the building fund."

The following Sunday, however, Sister Baker came up to Mary Lee again. "Please take these," she said, putting two pennies in Mary Lee's hand. "You've got to take them."

"What's this for?" Mary Lee asked, looking down at the two pennies.

"Well, I asked the Lord at the very beginning of the building program what I was to give," Sister Baker explained. "When I handed you that $135.05 last week I thought I had completed the pledge, but I went home and added it up and I was two pennies short."

By now Mary Lee's curiosity had gotten the best of her. "Sister Baker, how much did you pledge?" she asked.

"Seventy-five hundred dollars."

On a domestic's wages!

Our younger son Donnie wanted to give, but he didn't know just how to go about it. He had been married only a year and they were expecting their first baby. He had saved up a thousand dollars for the hospital maternity bill. One day the Lord said, *Donnie, what about that thousand dollars?*

"But Lord, what about the baby?"

I'll take care of the baby.

As it turned out, there were complications with the birth. The baby remained in intensive care ten days and Marion, Donnie's wife, had to return to the hospital after some of the placenta was discovered still in her womb. The bills mounted steadily. Donnie was afraid even to ask how much they came to; his insurance covered only the first five hundred dollars.

He waited and waited for a bill. Finally after six months it came. The total cost was $4,035. It was stamped *Paid in Full*. The insurance company had paid the entire amount.

His older brother Virgil refinanced his home twice to contribute several thousand dollars to the building program. I still owned a couple acres of land near where we had our camp in Virginia. Selling that I was able to put a good sum into the fund as well. But soon I began feeling God directing me to do something more. I didn't know how to tell Mary Lee, but I felt God wanted us to sell our home. We had built the house thirteen years prior and we both loved and enjoyed it.

"John, I just don't know," she said when I told her my guidance. "We've sold the property and given that money to the building fund, and it was quite a bit. God will have to speak to me too if He wants the house."

I didn't press the issue. I knew God could speak to her as well as He could to me. Two months later she was ready. We sold the house to Congressman Litton from Missouri and were able to give $130,000 to the building fund.

Thirteen years previously when we built we had tried first to buy a lot in the quiet, lovely Crestwood area. There was an oral agreement among the neighbors, however, that any newcomer would have to be "passed on" by the Crestwood Committee. Our realtor went to see them, and then we waited and waited. No response. "John," Mary Lee would say, "I wonder why we haven't heard from the

Committee?" Finally the realtor called us: "I'm so sorry to have to tell you this, but the Crestwood Committee has turned you down for the lot you want to buy."

"Why? What's wrong with us?"

"Nothing. They say they checked you out and you have good credit standing. It's just that—they say you pastor a black congregation and they're afraid you would be inviting them over to your house."

Now, househunting once more, we found a home in Crestwood, a fifty-year-old Spanish-style house. But by this time Crestwood was an all-black neighborhood. Mary Lee and I laughed and said, "You reckon the neighbors are meeting to discuss what kind of friends we'll be having over?" On the contrary, the current residents were graciousness itself.

We were nearing the end of the building program, only months away from completion of the new church. Gallantly and sacrificially though people had given, however, we had reached the end of our financial resources. We needed $125,000 immediately, and I knew of no way to get the money. I couldn't ask our people to do more than they were already doing. As I prayed for direction, the strangest answer kept coming: *Go to Florida and ask your brother Maurice for the money.*

Maurice? Who bore an understandable grudge against the church—and an unreasoning prejudice against blacks? Maurice, overseer of the family business, and the one of all my brothers and sisters with whom I had the least comfortable relationship? I argued with the Lord for days, but of course He always wins, and at last I obeyed.

18

The New Evangel Temple

The flight to Largo seemed the longest trip I'd ever made. It had been more than twenty-five years since the family had overruled Maurice to give me a loan to build the Athens church. Now once again a church building program was in financial need, and again I was turning to Maurice.

In his sixties, Maurice still raced motorcycles, with which he also herded cows on his three-hundred acre farm. He made no secret of his low opinion of religion, blacks, and much else besides.

I'd phoned him I was coming, and he was standing out in front of his house when I drove up in my rented car. We shook hands and stood staring at each other for a moment.

"Let's go down to the café and get some coffee," I suggested.

"Fine with me," Maurice responded.

Over coffee I poured out my need. Once again I was the

little brother, looking hopefully to Maurice for help. As we talked, I saw his expression soften, heard his openness as he questioned me about the building program. The barricade that the years had erected between Maurice and me simply and astonishingly came crumbling down. God alone had seen the changes in both our hearts that opened the way to a new relationship.

But I needed the money now, and there were only a few banking hours left. We called our brother Virgil and asked him to meet us at the family bank.

Tall and solidly built, Maurice was always a commanding figure. "I want to see Sam," Maurice told a bank officer, referring to the bank president.

"Oh, Mr. Meares, he's out of the office for a little while."

"How long before he'll be back?"

"He should return in half-an-hour if you'd care to wait."

"We'll wait."

After thirty minutes Maurice decided we'd waited long enough.

"Is there anybody else back there to talk to?" he asked. "You got a vice-president or somebody back there?"

"Why, yes, Mr. Meares. If you'll just wait a minute I'll see if he's free."

Two minutes later we were ushered into Mr. Carter's office. "Mr. Meares, good to see you. How may I help you?"

"This is my brother John," Maurice said, nodding toward me. "He's down from Washington to get some money. He needs $125,000 and I'm ready to sign for it. So I'd like for you to give him the money."

Mr. Carter smiled.

"Why, Mr. Meares, we can't just give him money. He'll

have to fill out forms and the board will have to approve the loan and—"

Maurice was shaking his head vigorously. "You see, my brother's a preacher. He has one of the best churches in Washington and he's building a confounded beautiful new church. That's why he needs the money now."

The banker shifted in his seat. "Uh . . . what do you have for collateral?"

"I have a note here you're collecting on that's worth a lot more than $125,000."

"Fine, Mr. Meares, but—"

I could see my brother's face begin to flush, signaling the rise of a storm. Virgil saw it, too.

"Maurice," he whispered, "what about your bonds?"

The storm abated. "What bonds?" Maurice asked.

Virgil reminded him of the contents of a safety deposit box.

"Well, I'll be. I forgot all about them!" A few minutes later Maurice returned to Mr. Carter's office, arms full of bonds. As Mr. Carter checked them off, a couple were missing. "I must have dropped them," said Maurice. He retraced his steps and picked them up. Twenty minutes later I had my check for $125,000.

"Remember, Maurice," I said as I made my farewells, "you promised you'd come to Washington for the dedication service."

"I'll be there," he said.

Back in Washington, I had a lot of repenting to do. I'd done my share of thinking and even talking negatively about Maurice. Now I had to ask God's forgiveness and tell everyone what he had done for us.

On March 9, 1975, over two hundred ministers and friends from across the country and overseas attended dedication services for the new, three million-dollar

Evangel Temple. It stirred my heart to see David du Plessis, a white South African, worshiping with his black South African brother, apostle Nicholas Bengu.

True to his word, Maurice joined the rest of my family from Florida for the week-long dedication celebration—and appeared to be having the time of his life.

"What did you do to Maurice?" my sisters asked.

"Nothing," I said. "Why?"

"Because he's changed!" said Velma.

He seemed to be enjoying not only the long church services, but the congregation.

I had asked our members to give Maurice an extra-special welcome when he came. They all remembered.

"You must be Maurice," a lady would greet him.

"Yes, ma'am," my brother would reply, rising from his chair.

"Well, I just want to thank you for your support of Evangel Temple," the greeter would respond, giving my brother a big hug.

I guess Maurice must have been hugged by a hundred people that week. If he hadn't already changed, he was now. God has strange ways to bring two brothers together.

Through the years I'd noticed that black congregations would often move into churches that whites had vacated. I'd wanted not something "second-hand" for my people, but something they could be truly proud of. As a result, our new facilities had cost us around a million dollars more than I anticipated. Maybe the Lord didn't let us know it was going to total so much or we might never have had faith to begin building. The whole time we took out a loan of only $350,000; the rest of the three million had miraculously come through the hands of this faithful remnant of a congregation. Their determination and joyous giving had surpassed all I could imagine.

Right on the heels of such an immense victory, however, came a real trial of our faith. No one in this small flock—I least of all—had considered what it would cost for the upkeep of a building this size. Instead of a simple sanctuary with two doors, front and back, we now had a four-story, 50,000 square-foot building with 150 doors, and it was taking us some time just to know what floor was for what.

We had been used to a three hundred dollar monthly utility bill; now it was $2,000 or more. Whereas the mortgage payment on Georgia Avenue had been $653 a month, it was now $8,000. Soon bills began to pile up. We had given and borrowed, stretched our faith, been obedient to what we felt the Lord had told us to give. Now our resources were exhausted. We still were running around three hundred at a service, which looked mighty small in this 2,000-seat auditorium. "Lord, what do we do now?"

Clarence Graves, one of the elders, put my attitude about our money problems into perspective. Now in his seventies, Clarence had been sixty-five years old before he accepted Christ into his life. In his teens he had moved from North Carolina to Washington. For twelve years he'd worked as a dining car waiter, then become a chauffeur to numerous government officials and VIP's traveling a lot, seeing a lot, and not giving God a thought. He hadn't been to church since he'd gone as a little boy with his grandmother.

In 1967 he had had a dream in which he saw himself at Evangel Temple. For the next two days the Lord kept dealing with him, reminding him of the way he was living and his excessive drinking. He couldn't get Evangel Temple out of his mind, so that Sunday he came, sitting in the back of the church just to watch. One of the Bible verses quoted that day was, "Everything that can be shaken will be shaken." "Lord," he whispered, "I just got

145

here. Please don't shake me off." That morning he cried during the entire service. Each time he came back after that he moved a little closer to the front, bringing extra handkerchiefs to take care of the tears. Eventually it happened. He surrendered his life to God and today is known as "the beloved elder."

Now Clarence, a few years later, thought I needed a word of advice concerning our financial situation.

"Pastor, I know you're concerned about not being able to pay the bills," he said, a look of mischief in his eyes. "Just accept this experience as a blessing from the Lord to help you identify with your congregation." Puzzled, I waited for him to explain. "Black people experience financial problems all the time," he said. "Now you know how it feels to be black."

I needed that. From that moment on I began to accept financial pressures as an expected part of existence. We began saying to ourselves, "We're going to make it." And make it we did, keeping at it until our bills were paid up.

Visiting ministers had prophesied that people would come to us "from the North, from the South, from the East, and from the West." At first we accepted this on faith alone, for it was two years before that huge auditorium began to fill up. Then it happened seemingly overnight. The balcony overflowed and we had to go to two Sunday morning services.

The choir, which at one time disbanded because I felt they were not ministering but entertaining, had now become skilled at leading people into worship. Today they're asked to sing for many functions here and in other cities; only if they can glorify God will they accept an invitation.

It was not uncommon for the people to say, "The first time I walked into Evangel Temple, I felt loved." The

146

worship and the teaching were bearing fruit. We were enjoying a harvest.

We added more elders to the staff, ordained over a hundred deacons to help us take care of the people that were being added to the church, while I stressed the believer's role in the world around us. "Whatever you do, do it as unto the Lord," I often say from the pulpit.

My joy through the years has been to see the poor, the hurting, the disenfranchised become confident, responsible, productive people in their community as well as in the Kingdom of God. What fulfillment to see lives changed! Divorced couples reunited. Drug addicts freed. Homosexuals delivered. People living out their dreams to start their own businesses. We have living examples of the power of the Gospel to change hearts and lives.

It was during a banquet at Washington's Sheraton Hotel to celebrate the church's thirtieth anniversary that Mary Lee and I were made aware of how far the Lord had brought us. Looking out over the fifteen hundred friends gathered for this special evening we saw a people who knew who they were and what their purpose was in life.

One young girl in particular, as she came up to take a picture of Mary Lee and me, was radiant and beautiful and feminine. She had started coming to Evangel Temple only two years earlier, hair cropped short, dressed in shorts, a militant lesbian. After she came forward for salvation her battle with the devil really began. For six months she was up and down, while the saints loved her and prayed with her and encouraged her until she became steady in the boat. As she left our table now, Mary Lee leaned over to me with tears trickling down her cheeks and said, "That's the power of the Gospel."

We spotted the young mother who'd begun coming to Evangel just after we moved into the new facilities. She had two small children, no husband. The Lord graciously saved her, but after some months we began to miss her. When I did see her it was in a store. "We haven't seen you lately," I said.

"Pastor, I couldn't come back. I'm too ashamed."

It was obvious that she was once again with child. "You need us now more than ever," I said. "Come back and let us love you and your child."

She returned to church. One evening in the Wednesday night prayer service she asked if she could say something. "I want to make an announcement," she said. "I am going off welfare. I am going to study to become a nurse." Today she works in one of our leading hospitals, sings in the choir, and never misses a service.

A few tables away we saw Richard Ashby. When he came to a Sunday morning service and saw a white man in the pulpit, he'd been ready to leave. Instead, he was wonderfully saved and filled with the Spirit. He immediately got involved in everything. Anything there was to do, Richard would do it. One day one of the members said, "Richard, you're on all the committees serving one way or another." He said, "That's right. When I was serving the devil I was on the lying committee, the stealing committee, the drug committee, the adultery committee, every committee the devil had. So I sure want to be on all of God's committees."

We saw another of our great soulwinners, Dorthea Lawson, a middle-aged woman who was once a street lady. She goes where they are and brings them to church.

That evening we saw a church full of people whose thinking had been transformed. When we started in 1955 we had only domestics and day workers; today our young people are graduating from college. We have doctors, dentists, lawyers, men in the Secret Service, people who own their own businesses. Welfare is not the answer. Christ is the answer.

*   *   *

One morning around 2:30 A.M. the phone rang. I wondered who in the world would be calling at this time of night.

"Pastor, it's me, Johnny."

It had been twelve years since he and Ethel had left Evangel Temple. Though I had rarely heard from him directly, I'd learned that his ministry had foundered, along with some of his business ventures and even his marriage.

Thirty minutes later Johnny was sitting across from me in our living room, looking tired and worn.

"I've been fasting and praying for a number of months," he said, "and I know that to be faithful to God I have to come back and submit my life to your spiritual leadership. I'm being obedient to the Lord in coming here. However, you're not obligated to take me back."

I knew this was difficult for Johnny to say. I didn't give him an answer right away. I first asked Mary Lee if she thought we should take him back and without hesitation she said, "Yes." Then I went to each of the elders and they all said, "Yes."

A lot had changed at Evangel Temple since Johnny and Ethel had left. We were no longer just a healing and revival church. Some roots and spiritual foundations had been laid; our structure had changed. There was a lot of catching up for Johnny to do when he returned. Nine months later in a Sunday night service the Lord told us all, "Now is the time for Johnny to again be a pastor and elder in this church."

19

Bind Us Together

◆◇ From the start of my ministry in Washington many young men with the call of God on their lives had asked me to be their bishop—in our tradition a shepherd or guide recognized as such by other shepherds. I'd felt unprepared and unable to meet the leadership responsibilities inherent in such a role, so I'd always declined.

In 1982 Bishop Bob McAllister of Rio de Janeiro, Brazil, came to spend a weekend with us. "John," he said, "you should be consecrated a bishop. Not only have you pastored this one church for twenty-seven years, but many other pastors outside of this local assembly look to you as their father in the Lord."

"Bob," I finally said, "you talk to my elders and see what they say. If they approve the idea, then it can be presented to the congregation."

Bob spoke to the elders, then during his sermon on Sunday morning made a statement that struck me like lightning. "This church will never go any farther in its spiritual growth," he said, "until you recognize Pastor Meares as your spiritual leader in the way he is recognized by many religious leaders around the country and overseas."

He went on to observe that I was recognized as a bishop (based on 1 Timothy 3) through the ministries I had served in Europe, Africa, South America, and many of the islands. But I was barely listening to him. Could it be that I was holding back Evangel Temple's progress because of my failure to accept spiritual responsibility? The office of bishop does not make the man, of course. Rather the man is reflected in the manner in which he relates to those around him.

I was recalled from my thoughts by the congregation standing on its feet, applauding thunderously. "Then two weeks from now on November 7," Bob said, "we will consecrate Pastor Meares as bishop."

On November 7, 1982, clergymen from all over came to be present for the consecration service. Nicholas Bengu came from South Africa, Silvano Lillie from Italy, David du Plessis from California, Earl Paulk from Atlanta—fifty or more ministers were present, with extra chairs set up for the overflow crowd. I couldn't believe it.

There was definitely an impartation that day as hands were laid on me. I saw my ministry come into focus as never before. Looking back, I realized that we had in fact reached out and built churches overseas. We'd helped support missionaries in many parts of the world. I'd participated in the Roman Catholic-Pentecostal dialogue, and was currently president of the International Evangelical Church and Missionary Association, a nondenominational fellowship of more than four hundred churches.

But our principal contribution was to come in another area. Tom Skinner, a former chaplain for the Washington

Redskins and noted black evangelist, was preaching for us in the latter part of 1983. "John," he said over lunch one day, "why do you keep it a secret what God is doing for you here?"

"What do you mean, Tom?"

"Our black churches need to see what's happening here. They need to feel the love, see the servant spirit, experience the worship—the whole thing." I listened as he continued to talk.

"You can provide vision, guidance, and encouragement for our ministers. They need to come see for themselves what God is doing here."

"What do I do?" I asked.

"Open up your church to them," he said. "You can be a showcase for other inner-city pastors whose churches are stalemated."

Our first Inner-City Pastors' Conference was held in March 1984. Up until the last day for registration I wondered how many would come. My question was answered on the final day when the responses tripled. Around three hundred ministers, most of them black, came from thirty-eight different states as well as Canada, Jamaica, Italy, and Bermuda. God blessed us with great conference speakers, workshops and times of fellowship. Practically all of our deacons took their vacations that week just so they could serve the delegates to the conference.

I was amazed that these black pastors would come to a white pastor to learn how to develop their ministries. A few came with misgivings. "When I saw two thousand black people worshiping God and this white man sitting on the platform," said a pastor from the Midwest, "I thought, *What am I getting into?*"

After a service or two our visitors had to admit we were for real. Real in our worship. Real in our love for each other. Real in our serving one another. We were just a real-people church.

Each year thereafter more pastors and leaders started coming to the conference. Our 1987 Inner-City Conference had just under a thousand registrants. They were here from forty-eight states, and many foreign countries, with at least two hundred white ministers among the registrants.

Every speaker was superb. But to me the most meaningful moment came after the Rev. Jack Hayford spoke on "reconciliation," the theme of the conference. At the conclusion of his message Jack asked the Reverend Luther Blackwell from Ohio to come to the pulpit so that they could break bread and take Communion together. Representing the white evangelical church, Jack knelt down and asked Brother Blackwell to forgive him for being insensitive to the hurts and the wrongs of the whites towards the blacks. He said, "So many of us just didn't know. . . ."

Then Luther Blackwell knelt and asked Jack to forgive him and the black church for the hard feelings, the hatred, the unforgiveness they had held in their hearts toward the whites.

There was hardly a dry eye in the congregation. There were black South Africans hugging white South Africans, asking each other's forgiveness. Ancient prejudices were being laid aside, walls beginning to crumble. That day I saw my ministry more clearly than ever as one of reconciliation between the white church and the black church.

Because of our continued growth it was obvious that we needed larger facilities. Our parking problems alone were becoming impossible and we knew we had to do something. There were twelve acres of ground directly behind and to one side of the church that we thought maybe we could buy. I went to work, contacting the owners, doing everything I could to arrange the purchase. I flew to Florida to see the principal owners and made them an offer of more than three million dollars. They turned it down. We tried every angle we knew and got nowhere. Was God shutting the door, saying, *This ground is not for you?* It seemed so. Soon a sign went up on the property saying, *Edgewood Shopping Center coming soon.*

Ministers would say, "If you want to keep on growing, you're going to have to move where there is more land." Others would say, "Why don't you move out of the city?" Our sons too suggested this, but neither Mary Lee nor I would entertain the thought. God had put us in the inner city!

It was not until a minister visiting from Korea, Paul Yonggi Cho, prophesied that we were to move out—"far enough to have sufficient ground to do what the Lord wants to do through you"—that the thing rang true in both Mary Lee's and my spirits as well as in the spirits of the congregation.

When we began to take stock, more than half of our members already lived in Maryland and were driving twenty, thirty minutes, as much as an hour, to come to church. Property in Washington had so skyrocketed in value that it was forcing people to move to the suburbs. A rowhouse that once sold for $20,000 now brought $130,000 or more. It was hardly feasible for families to live in Washington.

As we prayed week by week we asked the Lord for seven things:

1. One hundred acres or more.
2. Not more than one million dollars for one hundred acres.
3. Plenty of parking space.
4. Favor with the community.
5. Visibility.

6. Availability.
7. Landmarks to identify the location.

I contacted a land appraiser, giving him a description of what we needed. He showed us several parcels of ground, but none of them met our seven conditions. Then one day I went to his office and looked with him in his real estate plat book. He pointed to a parcel of ground on Central Avenue that he thought was for sale. I studied the lay of the ground and said, "No, that isn't suitable, but the property across the street looks ideal."

He told me that piece of land had never been for sale. It had been left in a trust to an Episcopal church but there were so many restrictions on it that the church couldn't use it.

After I left his office I drove around this property and had an experience I had never had before. I was so overwhelmed with the presence of God I could hardly drive my car. To me this was affirmation that this was in fact the property God wanted us to have.

When I reached the house that evening Mary Lee had dinner on the table. I said, "Honey, do you mind if I don't eat? I'd really like to spend the evening alone in the guest room." She understood.

I told my elders of the experience I had and they got excited with me. We went out to the property and prayed over it, claiming it as ours.

Then I went back to the appraiser but he still said, "It can't be bought."

I asked him to get in touch with the trustees and present them a contract anyway. Several months later, after several contracts had been presented, we had made no headway. Finally I took three of my elders with me to see the officers of the trust. During that meeting we made a verbal offer of a price and they verbally accepted. More months passed while we negotiated the terms of the contract, and continued to pray and believe. Altogether it was a year-and-a-half before the details were ironed out.

One of the seven things we had asked the Lord for was "one hundred acres or more." The owners would not sell one hundred acres. It was all or none, and that "all" meant 462 acres! We really had to stretch our faith to visualize 462 acres of property. Our present facilities covered a little over half an acre. But the asking price was only $1,500,000. We had asked the Lord for a hundred acres for a million dollars. The Lord had done abundantly above all that we could ask or think.

Joyfully we went to the closing: the property was now Evangel Temple's, debt-free, paid in full. The property is located on Central and Church Roads, ten miles due east of the Capitol building in the heart of the rapidly expanding megaplex of Washington, Baltimore, and Annapolis. In a couple of decades this large piece of ground may well again be the inner city of these three adjoining metropolises. We're presently completing plans for a four thousand-seat sanctuary.

To persons visiting Evangel Temple for the first time, it may seem that it has always been the loving, worshiping church they see now. But this is not the case. God does not specialize in overnight successes. He is interested in growth from the ground up, laying a firm foundation with Jesus Christ as the Chief Cornerstone. The level of maturity expressed through the ministry of Evangel Temple today has been achieved through a growth process lasting thirty-two years.

There is a danger sometimes when blessings are poured out as freely as they have been upon us, that we may come to take them for granted, forgetting one blessing as soon as we receive the next. But the past remains part of our lives, part of ourselves. Our history serves as a mirror, and as we peer into it, we will be able to see our growth from God's perspective, acquiring an appreciation for the rich heritage which is ours in Him.

One of the rich heritages for Mary Lee and me has been for the Lord to call both our sons, Virgil and Donnie, and their wives, and our daughter, Cynthia, to work with us. Where they are in their own Abrahamic journeys, what distances, spiritual or intellectual, they have traveled and have still to travel from their roots in us, God and they are working out. In the meantime it is an immeasurable blessing for Mary Lee and me to work together with them as a family.

And as a larger family in Him. I believe God has faithfully, patiently, and purposefully brought to fruition the plan He ordained from the beginning of time for this particular body of believers. From the very beginning, from the tent on Benning Road (where the RFK Stadium now stands) to the present time, we have seen the hand of God knit us into a united congregation numbering today over three thousand members.

As you approach your seventies it becomes more important than ever to get your marching orders straight. Every ministry has its God-ordained destiny. I believe the destiny of Evangel Temple is to be a force of reconciliation, to bind together black and white ministers, black and white churches, black and white people.

Why should there be a black church and a white church? Does God have two churches? Acts 17:26 reads: "From one man [God] made every nation of men, that they should inhabit the whole earth. . . ." Are we not one body of believers?

157

I really feel that until God has His one Church—the black church and the white church recognizing one another as family in Christ—we will not be the spiritual force we are supposed to be in the world.

Racism is rarely talked about or acknowledged by the Church. Historically, the Church played a big part in entrenching segregation in American society. Now it is time for us as ministers of the Gospel to accept our responsibility for the division of the Church.

We zealously support missions overseas but hardly give a thought to the needs of those different from us in our own towns and cities. Our government brought about integration, but only the Church can bring reconciliation. This split is the logjam, the bar to revival. Once it is dealt with, the Holy Spirit will unloose the logs and allow the river of praise to flow. Racism is harmful not only when expressed in violence; it is also harmful when expressed through neglect.

My greatest desire and vision now is to see us be bound together. Just as it was the Spirit who broke down denominational walls and let us see each other as brothers and sisters in Christ, let us pray for the walls of racism to be torn down until the prayer of Jesus, "That they may be one," is brought to fulfillment.

Of the many precious saints and charter members of Evangel Temple, one of the most beloved was Mama White. She was a dear fervent prayer warrior who loved God with all her heart. She could neither read nor write, but she so longed to read the Bible. One day she said, "Lord, please let me read Your Word." God answered that prayer. She could not read one word of a newspaper, but when she picked up the Bible she could read.

So many times during services she would get so happy she could no longer remain in her seat. She would make her way out into the aisle and walk up and down praising God for His goodness. After a few minutes of this she would end her testimony with these words: "When you pray, don't pray for me. Just pray for the Church—for I's in there somewhere!"